The Tantra of Great Bliss

And

The Tantra of the Natural Intent of the Heart

With Tibetan Texts

Translations by

Christopher Wilkinson

Published by Christopher Wilkinson

Cambridge, MA, USA

ISBN: 1517225485
ISBN-13: 978-1517225483

DEDICATION

To Vairochana the translator,

In thanks for your life's good work.

CONTENTS

ACKNOWLEDGMENTS

First and foremost, I wish to thank my root teacher Dezhung Rinpoche for constantly bringing out the best in me and encouraging me to pursue a comprehension of every branch of Buddhist learning. It was he who introduced me to Dilgo Kyentse Rinpoche, and through his recommendations enabled me to receive full empowerments, transmissions, and permissions in the areas of Mahā, Anu, and Ati Yogas. With the highest regard I wish to thank Dilgo Kyentse Rinpoche, Khetsun Zangpo Rinpoche, Nyoshul Khen Rinpoche, and Khenpo Palden Sherab for their kind instruction and encouragement in my effort to translate the literature of the rDzogs chen. There are many individuals, too many to name here, that have helped me over the years to become a qualified translator, in many ways. At this time I want to remember the kindness of Ngawang Kunga Trinlay Sakyapa, Jigdral Dagchen Sakya Rinpoche, Dhongthog Rinpoche, H.H. Karmapa Rangjung Rigpay Dorje, Kalu Rinpoche, Chogyam Trungpa Rinpoche, Geshe Ngawang Nornang, Carl Potter, David Ruegg, Turrell Wylie, Gene Smith, Karen Lang, Richard Solomon, Jack Hawley, David Jackson, Cyrus Stearns, Herbert Guenther, Eva Neumeier-Dargyay, Leslie Kawamura, Robert Thurman, Paul Nietupski, Lou Lancaster, David Snellgrove, Jean-Luc Achard, Steve Landsberg, Moke Mokotoff, Tsultrim Alione, Carolyn Klein, Rob Mayer, Jonathan Silk, David White, Mark Tatz, Steve Goodman, and Kennard Lipman. I want to make special thanks to Sarah Moosvi for proofing the manuscript. The many people who have contributed to my understanding and ability to do this work cannot be counted. I wish to thank everyone that has taken a kind interest in these translations, however slight, for your part in making this work a reality.

.

INTRODUCTION

The teachings of Vajrasattva's Magnificent Sky belong to the Great Perfection transmission of esoteric Buddhism, also known as *Atiyoga*. This tradition is based on an instantaneous approach to enlightenment, one in which there is no practice or meditation. The Guhyagarbha Tantra is the primary source work for the Mahāyoga transmission, where visualizations, mantras, mandalas, and practices are primary. The Atiyoga teaches instantaneous enlightenment, while the Mahāyoga teaches profound means for attaining enlightenment quickly. The two Tantras translated in this volume offer us an insight into the interrelationship of these two classes of Tantra as they are brought together. Starting out with the inspiration of the Atiyoga, we are gradually introduced to a seed syllable and then to mandalas both physical and sonic, elaborately described in colorful detail. Practices are described, including a graphic description of sexual yoga. Then we are reminded that there is no practice or meditation.

A central theme in the Tantra of Great Bliss is "generation." Generation is generally understood in Vajrayana Buddhism to be that part of a meditation practice in which the practitioner "generates" a mandala or a deity by an act of visualization. In the Mahāyoga, generation is followed by "perfection," or "completion." Generation and perfection are the two stages of any Mahāyoga practice. Generation is a word for giving birth to something, in this case, a visualization. This practice usually includes the beaming out and reconvening of lights, a kind of expansion and contraction. This Tantra denounces all visualization practices, but recognizes a playfulness in which we may generate mandalas, hinting at a perfection that is not a practice, but is what we are. It would seem, then, that even in the Great Perfection there is generation, but it is not considered to be a stage of anything.

The translations in this book were done based on Tibetan manuscripts. The Indian source works have been lost in time. The Tibetan texts we have are translations made by Vairochana, a famous Tibetan translator who went to India in search of the literature on instantaneous enlightenment in the Eighth Century of our era. His biography[1] recounts his finding a teacher, Śrī Singha, who had the transmission, but did not have the books, as the King had put them under lock and seal due to a disturbance involving a prostitute and a nun.[2] So Śrī Singha and Vairochana broke in to the palace by night, broke the seals, and stole the books. Then, over a period of many years, Vairochana studied these texts under Śrī Singha. As we have seen in the case of The Great Tantra of Vajrasattva,[3] Vairochana was actively translating literature while with his teacher in Dhahena. The Tantra of Great Bliss, as recorded at the end of the book, was also translated by Vairochana in the company of Śrī Singha. It is certain that Vairochana carried finished translations of several works with him when he returned to his country. On return to Tibet, however, he had a difficult time at court, and was soon exiled to Tsawarong, a remote area, where he spent the rest of his life translating. His biography tells us that his difficulties at court were on account of demands from India that he be executed, which came with statements that his translations were only of minor magical works. Vairochana himself admits that even during his lifetime inquiries were being made into the authenticity of the works he translated.[4]

Vairochana had gone to India in search of teachings on instantaneous enlightenment, which was a very hot topic in Tibet at that time. Tibetans of the day were very concerned about whether enlightenment was a gradual process or an instantaneous realization. By the last decade of the Eighth Century, this concern led up to the famous Samye debates, in which the Chinese Hvashang took the instantaneous position and the Indian Kamalashila took the gradual one. In Tibetan history, the instantaneous approach is associated with China, while the gradual approach is associated with India, even though Vairochana's translations clearly show that there was a solid Indian transmission of the instantaneous approach.

One of the primary arguments against the instantaneous approach is that it fails to account for karma, or any cause and result relationship, which leads to moral depravity. In the Tantra of Great Bliss we find descriptions of practices that are disgusting, unhealthy, immoral, and even illegal, in tandem with profound explications of a wisdom that is to be understood instantaneously. We cannot be sure whether these descriptions are meant to be taken literally or figuratively, whether they are inserted only for their shock value, or were actually to be practiced. We can be sure, however, that even during Vairochana's times these kinds of statements would have been taken as representative of an immorality that is not to be associated with Buddhism as we usually understand the tradition. We can also be sure that these are among the reasons that the gradual approach is said to have won the Samye debates. There is no direct evidence that Vairochana was banished to Tsawarong on account of the content of his literary output, but we may wonder if it was found undesirable at court to have the Indian position associated with such practices at a time when it stood for morality, education, and social order, as much as for enlightenment. It is not impossible that Vairochana was exiled to Tsawarong precisely so that he would not be present at the Samye debates.

The Tantras here translated are among the source works that inspired such great Tibetan luminaries as Longchen Rabjampa (1308-1364), Jigme Lingpa (1729-1798), and Mipham Gyatso (1846-1912). It is clear that the thinking within these Tantras was found critical to an understanding of the profundities of the Great Perfection, even hundreds of years after Vairochana's translation, and that those who sought to reconcile the inspiration of the Great Perfection with the practical realities of a practicing path, such as the Mahāyoga, found these Tantras to be critical to their understanding. In translating these works, I do not endorse the practices described within, but by translating them into English I hope to provide modern readers access to these important contributions to the literary heritage of mankind, empowering you to read, discuss, evaluate, and ponder these source works yourselves, just as the great thinkers of the Tibetan tradition have done for these many centuries.

We might wonder whether it is due to the influence of the Guhyagarbha that The Tantra of Great Bliss recommends evil practices. The second Tantra in this book, The Tantra on the Secret Intent of the Heart also brings together the Atiyoga of the Magnificent Sky tradition and the Mahāyoga of the Guhyagarbha, but is not so explicit in words that might offend. We will gain a more holistic understanding of the tradition by reading both. There are currently a few scholars and translators bringing out good work on the Guhyagarbha Tantra and its transmission. I do not pretend to be capable of contrasting or comparing these Tantras of the Magnificent Sky transmission with that of the Guhyagarbha Tantra, while I do hope that my translations here will be found useful by those who study and practice the Guhyagarbha, and that further work will be done in this area.

The Tantra of Great Bliss recommends itself for the likes of butchers, prostitutes, and evil doers, but is written in a literary style that we would only expect from highly educated people. It frequently compares its own insights to those of the Rishis, the seers who were the original authors of the Vedas, encouraging us to surmise that these Tantras were written by members of the caste of Brahmins. The Tantra comes to us from out of the same basic time period as the works of Saraha, and it does discuss the Mahamudra at numerous points. Those who study the early roots of the Mahamudra transmission and its relationship to the Great Perfection transmission will find these Tantras helpful.

The Kunche Gyalpo, or All-Creating King, an important source work for the Great Perfection, has fifty-five verses in its thirtieth chapter, with a colophon that calls these verses Vajrasattva's Magnificent Sky. I have long believed that these fifty-five verses were excerpted from out of the many Magnificent Sky Tantras.[5] It is now clear that the majority of these fifty-five verses, if not all of them, are to be found in the Tantra of Great Bliss. What is really needed at this time is a critical edition of all of these texts which can be cross-checked for shared content between texts and inter-textualities. The current evolution of computer technology promises us much assistance in developing such editions, as the comparison of numerous manuscripts will soon be possible with only a few clicks of the mouse, and search engines are rapidly being deployed by which textual variants do not prevent matches. Rather than spend long hours doing this work at this time, I postpone the effort till this new technology may be implemented in classical Tibetan studies.

The Tantra of Great Bliss is so titled at the end of each of the chapters of its contents, while it has numerous titles attributed to it at the beginning and at the end of the book. The Tantra of the Natural Intent of the Heart is also so titled in the chapter colophons. These Tantras are to be found in the collections of ancient literature that are collectively known as Nyingma Gyubum, or Hundred Thousand Tantras of the Ancients. There are several of these collections extant. I have done these translations using the mTshams brag manuscript,[6] where they are found on pages 415 to 529 of the second volume. In an effort to help preserve these ancient writings, and as an aid to those who wish to check the original, images of the pages are included at the end of this book.

The Tantra of Great Bliss is clearly stated to have been translated by both Śrī Singha and Vairochana. The Tantra of the Secret Intent of the Heart does not offer the names of any translators. A manuscript witness of the text is also found in the Hundred Thousand Tantras of Vairochana,[7] however, which assures us that the tradition believes it have been translated by Vairochana.

I have made every effort to translate into a standard of English that educated readers from around the world will find accessible. I have approached the text primarily as a work of literature, and have avoided the jargon often associated with philosophical inquiry, striving to be true to the original text while retaining literary quality. In cases where there are technical terms that I believe need more study, I have noted them. I hope that these translations provide the English speaking world with a window into the arcane world of this amazing literature, so that it may be better understood and appreciated.

When it comes to preserving the literary heritage of mankind, we are at a time of crisis. Vast repositories of literature are being lost due to inattentiveness, the burning of libraries, and the failure to maintain knowledge of the works that our ancestors spent their lives in producing. Tibet alone has a massive literary heritage, with over thirteen centuries of concentrated literary output. The ancient Tantras are works that Tibetans gathered from outside of Tibet and translated, from very early on, as part of a general acquisition of knowledge by the Tibetan dynastic empire. At this time we do not even have a comprehensive and accessible catalogue of all the titles of the works translated into Tibetan during this period. We cannot even estimate the possibilities here as per the survival of literature thought to have been lost by mankind. To give you an idea of the extent of this: The great manuscript collections of ancient literature available today include the Hundred Thousand Tantras of the Ancients, the mTshams brag manuscript of which contains forty-six volumes of about a thousand pages each. The Dege xylograph edition has twenty-six volumes. The Vairo rGyud 'bum, The Hundred Thousand Tantras of Vairochana, has eight volumes. Another important collection of ancient Tantras is the bKa' ma shin tu rgyas pa, of which there are four extant versions ranging from 110 to 137 volumes in length, each. The amount of this literature that has so far been translated into any modern language is probably less than one volume. We are just beginning to scratch the surface of this store of ancient wisdom. I hope that my translations will serve to attract attention to this trove of literature, and that more and better translations and studies will be made in the coming future.

It is certain that scholars of the future will find shortcomings in my work, and what I have done may well be a mere stepping stone toward greater understanding. At the time of this writing there are only a handful of people on Earth seriously studying and translating this literature. I hope that my readers develop a taste for these works, and that younger scholars will be inspired to investigate these vast literary treasures preserved in Tibet. I also hope that the attention my translations do gain serves to encourage members of the Tibetan community to actively delve into these literary treasures from their past, as there are very few living Tibetans who concern themselves with the early translations at this time. I also hope that those who study the thought of India will be pleased to have restored to them, even in modern English, these important contributions to the history of Indian thought.

THE TANTRA OF GREAT BLISS

In the Indian Language:

Vajrasatva Khasya Mahā Samantabhadra Guhya Garbha Tantra

In the Tibetan Language:

rDo rje sems dpa' nam mkha' che kun tu bzang po

gSang ba snying po'i rgyud

In the English Language:

The Tantra of the Secret Heart

Of the All Good Vajrasattva's Magnificent Sky

The Tantra of Great Bliss

THE BASIC SCENE FOR THE SECRET UPADEŚA

I bow to the Blessed One,
The glorious All Good One.

I heard these words on one occasion:

The Blessed One, the Tathagata, the completely perfected Buddha, the very soul[1] of the vajra body, speech, and mind of all the Blessed Tathagatas of the ten directions and of the four times, being no different than any Buddha, none excepted, is a great compassionate one, for he has the precious jewel of great compassion and enjoys the perfection that originates in generation.[2] This the great compassion of a Tathagata.

The finest place to abide
Is where there are many kinds of non-abiding.
The special quality of Akaniṣṭa
Is that it has no border or center,
Yet it is a defined area.
It has four corners,
And there are four doors on its surface.

A ladder of thoughts and ideas
Wraps around the vase.
There is a wheel with spokes.
Its foundation has no measure.
Its ornaments are inconceivable.

---

[1] bDag nyid, Ātmatā
[2] A reference to Generation stage yoga.

3

There is a net with hanging brocade,
Where five kinds of lotuses blaze
With five lights.
It has inconceivable ornamentation,
Both outside and inside.

At its center there is a lion on a lotus.
On an altar of blazing jewels,
The heart-essence of the holy truth
Is entwined with the unsurpassed.

The wheel has four spokes of blazing light.
Their special quality is a supreme perfection.
This is how samadhi retains samadhi.

The blazing mandala is like this:
The mandala of the thirty-two is unsurpassed.

A blazing light of great compassion shone
In the palace of Zomopuri,
Holding the hearts of those who are mature,
And at that very moment,
A crown jewel of words that are definite
Blazed forth!
The Blessed One used the tip of his tongue
To brilliantly make public,
For the audience of Brilliant Vision[3] and the rest,
This great secret.

Those who dwell in the fullness of brilliant certainty
Are Blessed Ones,
For this exists naturally
In all living things.

Even though we might made attributions about it,
Due to our own revertedness,
This is none other than
Self-originating liberation.

---

[3] Rab snang

This heart-essence is not something to seek.
It is not something that is non-existent.
It has the heart of a vajra.
It is not something that exists.
It has the heart of non-existence.

The sufferings of living beings
Are totally infused with the Bodhicitta,
So they are its play.
We have no regrets about that,
For we dwell in an equanimity
That is like the end of the sky.

Then the Blessed One Vajra Heart[4] entered the equanimity of samadhi, and spoke out with this intentional statement:

There is no discussion.
Those who dwell in this,
The supreme solidity of a vajra heart,
Retain the mandala of vajra wisdom.

These yogins are fortunate.
They separate their own objectives
From those of others,
And play among the spontaneously made
Objects of illusion.

The embodiment of the Dharma
Encompasses all things.
That is why this mandala is not separate
From any other.
It is the equal of all the Buddhas.
It is the embodiment of excellence,
And is endowed with all its forms.

From the Tantra of Great Bliss,[5] this is chapter one: The Basic Scene for the Secret Upadeśa.

---

[4] rDo rje snying po
[5] bDe ba chen po'i rgyud

TEACHING
THAT THE HEART-ESSENCE
OF THE SECRET UPADEŚA
IS IN FACT THE GREAT PERFECTION

Then again the Blessed One entered the samadhi of primordial liberation, and spoke out with this intentional statement:

The path of primordial liberation
Is that we are entirely free from every evil
Done by seeing, hearing, touching, or remembering
The mandala of the truth itself.
This is the heart-essence of spontaneously-realized Buddhahood!

Nothing exceeds it.
It is entirely perfect.
It is unchanging.
It dwells in honesty.
It is easy and difficult.
It is difficult because it is easy.

It is not to be perceived directly.
It encompasses everything.
Vajrasattva has not exemplified
Any teaching that says:
"This is to be perceived directly."

The great bliss that is spontaneously present
Is not measured or exemplified
By things like our costumes or our making things blaze,
So we will not see
The mandala of the Buddha
By merely acquiring a seal.

All the enumerations,
However many there may be,
With no exceptions,
Are causes of ensnarement.
They are obstructions to enlightenment.

In true enlightenment,
There is no enlightenment.

So it is that the Buddha's Dharma
Also does not exist.
We are liberated from virtue and evil.
We have no practice, view, applications,
Or anything else.
We have no conventionalities made of words,
For this transcends the topics of dominion and wisdom.

Self-originating wisdom is not to be sought.

There is an unsurpassed bliss
In the mind that seeks
For things that are a union
Of appearance and desire,
But this is obstructed by that,
And there are big problems.

Our present happiness
And our future happiness
Are either directly perceived,
Or come to us from behind.
There are also problems with these.
We must not rely on them.

E Ma'o!
This is really most amazing.
That Buddhas come together

From something that is not to be exemplified in words
Is most amazing.

This vehicle is like the sky.
The space of viewpoints
Is strewn with charnel grounds.

Vajrasattva abides in happiness.
He has no ideas in reference to time.

This is beyond the paths that we travel on or apply.
On careful investigation,
A true significance for being
Does not exist.
There is nothing to call a view,
And there is no heart-essence.
We will not even get a name
For the sky.

In this way,
Like this,
And for this reason,
This is taught to this,
And it attains this.
This is the heart,
And this is why
It is most amazing
That this comes from this.

The this of the past,
The this of the present,
And likewise the grandness in the presence of this,
Are like this,
And resemble the path of this,
For this is the true nature of this.

Because this resembles this,
It is a path for everyone.
It has come to us from the moon,
Along with a parcel.

It is the equality of everything.
We will not succeed

By referring to it in terms of a position.

This is beyond the objects of our prayers.
We spontaneously achieve an excellent embodiment,
Without effort.
It is a state of unity,
Not to be divided by conventionalities.

Those who are delusional
Seek to enumerate conventionalities.
This is like putting things into the hands
Of those who were born blind.
We will not succeed at anything.
Without illumination,
Nothing will be achieved at all.

Then the Blessed One entered the equanimity of the samadhi of
extreme profundity, and spoke out with this intentional statement:

The summation of all things
Is a space for everyone.
It is like the mind of everyone.

A vajra is a summation of vajras.
It is the embodiment of great bliss.
Smooth equanimity is not compounded.
The dimension of equality is the highest greatness.

It is not to be visualized.
It is not born and does not end.
It is invisible.

This heart of excellence is holy.
It is not complicated.
There has never been any hope
Of acquiring it from some other Buddha.
This is the way that it is.

But even in the way that it is,
We do not visualize any middle way.
We do not maintain any two truths.
Those who keep to two truths
Do not even have an eighth level.

This is it:
That for which there is no sign
Is achieved spontaneously,
Without any effort.

There have never been any conventionalities
For counting
Maintained by the holy.
So how could there be a conventionality
For this heart-essence of the vehicles?

To have no conventionalities
Contradicts the desire for applicable views,
Doors of protection,
And results.

There is nothing whatever
About this heart of holiness
To be counted as a vehicle.

The desire for a vehicle
That we may search and count,
Is a space that we are to understand.

The desire to attain Buddhahood
As a result,
Is a delusional path.

Going to the end of the tenth level is,
In fact,
Clinging and conceptualizing.
In the clinging to ideas,
We do not dwell upon the profundity of the path.

There is no path.
Those who desire a path
Are delusional about where they are going.

There is no attainment.
Those who desire results
Do not see what is real.

We will not find the dominion of wisdom
By desiring this dominion.
We will not see the truth
By meditating on a mudra or a body.
We will not know the ocean's exhaustion,
By stirring it with a ladle.
We will not become Buddhas
By meditating on the apparent world as a mudra.
We will not become enlightened
By renouncing the good things we desire.
We will not find nirvana
By rejecting the five kinds of emotional problems.

Even if we use indestructible analogies of logic,
Such as: "When the eggs hatch, the baby birds fly,"
We will not find nirvana.

At the very moment
We hear of this unsought King,
Primordially royal and primordially present,
Who is not to be sought out through any vehicle,
Or referred to in any transmission of the Unwritten,[6]
Which is the indivisible truth of non-duality,
We are Buddhas.

The short path is an innocence
That does not seek.
This is the supreme embodiment
Of an unsurpassed King of Doctors,
For minds that are ill.

Until we see this,
We don't see anything.
To see the Buddhas,
Whose number is that of the sands,
Is not a vision in a dream.
On the side where we have woken up
From our lack of seeing,
We do not see anything at all.

---

[6] Yi ge med pa. This is the title of one of the Tantras in this class, translated in
Secret Sky: The Ancient Tantras on Vajrasattva's Magnificent Sky.

There are no atoms.
They are like things we see in the distance.
It is difficult to teach this
By saying: "This."

To discover the vision of this:
No matter what perfumed water
We pour into the ocean,
It is still the ocean.

There are no analogies
For the delusional belief
That wisdom is in objects.
It is a delusional vision.
Anyone who understands things this way
Is small in wisdom.

The wisdom of ignorance
Is a higher perception.
It is appropriate that we work on
The totality of our desires.
After we have worked on them a while
It is possible that we will see.

This heart-essence is the origin of all things,
Which nothing can hinder.
It manifests in a way by which
Without this there will not be that.

Those who study it,
Those who want for it,
Those who meditate on it in retreat,
Do not live with it.

The children of a king are royal,
From the beginning,
And so they remain.

Even the Buddha,
Who knows all things,
Will not find this
By searching for it.

Our true natures are unmoving,
By their very character,
And unshakable.
We have dwelt with them naturally
Since the beginning.

Who can see a view?
There are no views on this.
We will not encounter the signs
By carefully analyzing this topic with logic.

Baby garudas are the adversaries of lion cubs,
Right from the womb.
Just so,
This space of unchanging spaciousness
Is an adversary.

We want a path
That is the result of someone having searched through
And studied throughout all the vehicles,
But if we do not see
That this heart-essence of spaciousness
Is devoid of finery,
From the beginning,
Then we are like people
Who are looking from the ocean
At a river of water,
But die of thirst.

This heart-essence is a moon-water mirror.
It is luminous without being pointed out,
And no matter what happens,
We abide in it without moving.

An analogy is that this resembles
The situation in which
The highest royal banner
Is the standard of the king.

This is a superior vehicle.
It is the heart-essence of the vehicles.
An analogy is that this resembles
The situation in which

Without a sprout
A trunk will never come to be.

The river of bliss
Has never existed.
It is unborn,
And will not come to be.
If we do not see this,
We will never become Buddhas.

An analogy is that this resembles
The situation in which
The true nature of a sprout's fruition
Is a pomegranate.

This unborn, unsought, unattained heart-essence
Is the sprout
Of the Victorious Ones.
It is the fruition of Buddhahood.

There is nothing to be done.
There is no falling out of space.
This, therefore, is the best of rituals.

We remain in the way that it is,
Without searching for anything.
This is a space of meditation.
It is a path of purity,
A supreme path that is unsurpassed,
A path to the end.
It is our body.

The Victorious One himself
Absolutely does not have
Any heart-essence
That will appear in the future.

It is not necessary to chant.
Generating ourselves into bodies
Is a path for children.
The path that reaches the end
Does not teach that anything is real.
From the beginning,

This has been the supreme heart-essence of our mudra:
The cause is the result.

The Sutras, Vinaya, and Abhidharma
Are ornamented with a wisdom of total perfection.
It is a space of unstained spaciousness,
The completion of the accumulation of merit and wisdom.

Rishis and great meditators who want to meditate on this
Do not see it.
It is possible to engage in something we think we see,
But there is nothing there other than this.
It is difficult to see this clearly.
It is like the tributary waters seeking the ocean.

The critics divide this heart-essence of unity
Into vehicles.
The division into vehicles is, in fact,
This very thing.
We will not find a path
That is not this.
Even if we do find a path,
It will be the long road of delusion.
We will be like oxen stuck in the mud.

When a single leaf appears on a twig,
It is a refuge for the roots.
If this were absent,
It would not be possible for that to appear.
That is why this heart-essence of the Dharma
Is the root of excellence.

We fail at this
When we meditate excessively on a single body.
Meditating on two
Brings a lot of ideas and conclusions,
And these are enumerations.
Desire for them increases
When we depend on purity.

There is no enlightenment.
This is a long road.
We will not find the road to high status

By travelling over it as if it were a road.
That is a deviation.
It will be impossible for us to attain Buddhahood this way.
There is absolutely no enlightenment in it.

We want it,
But we do not abide in it.
This is the river of ideas.
The meaning will not be evident
To those who have ideas.
This is a great sorrow.

There never was
A placing of the wheel of delusion
Into equanimity.
There is nothing to take up or reject.
When we put enlightenment behind us,
We find it.
It is invisible.
It does not appear to anyone who desires enlightenment.

Reckonings of the earth are the concerns of children.
They do not find the most excellent of levels.
Those who hold to duality
Lack a heart of spaciousness.
They have a river of ideas.

Then the Blessed One entered the equanimity of the samadhi of
portent, and spoke out this intentional speech:

The three thousand worlds
Have never needed to be liberated.
They are primordially balanced
And primordially Buddhas.
They are primordially free from liberation.

A heart of excellence
Is an embodiment of the Mahamudra.[7]
The mind is, in fact, a vajra.
Nothing whatsoever can destroy it.
The Bodhicitta is a precious jewel.

---

[7] Phyag rgya chen po, the "Great Seal."

It may appear to be anything.

The sky is gold.
It is the fundament of the ocean.
The embodiment of total freedom
Is like the shining moon.

It is the sky that generates all things.
It is a wish-fulfilling tree.
With no exceptions,
And none left out,
It is the most excellent thing there is.
It pervades primordially,
And is primordially a Buddha.

There is no door to get through.
We basically do not desire
To attain some result
From applications, views, protections, and practices.
These desires are major obstructions
To this Great Perfection.

There is no place for us to find
By studying and searching.
There has never been any need to study.
The three realms are forever the Buddha.

It is impossible to use our senses
To cast this as a practice ground for words.
There are no instructions on this that say: "Meditate."
There is nothing to meditate on.
There is not even a word to exemplify it.
To accumulate wisdom,
Which has no dominion,
And speak of it with our voices,
Obstructs us.

This is not something that is not anything at all.
It has a heart-essence of non-existence.

No view,
No practice,
No protection,

No meditation:
This is the very heart.

Then Vajradhara asked him:

Blessed One,
How can something be perfected
From out of something that has no essence?

Then the Blessed One, the All Good One, entered the equanimity
of the samadhi in which all things are spontaneously perfected, and spoke
out intentionally on this topic:

Our own Bodhicitta is,
In fact,
The origin of all things.
Do not look for it anywhere else.

There has never been anything above it.
There are no conventionalities for talking about it.
It is enlightenment.

Everything is perfected in this jewel of the sky.
It may appear as anything at all.
This is why this very mandala
Is perfected in this,
Regardless of how the mandala may appear.

It is an essence that has no form.
It is like a water-moon.
An embodiment of form
May appear to be anything,
But it is perfected in this.
This is the heart-essence of existence.
All the Buddhas,
None excepted,
Are perfected in this.

This is the heart-essence of non-existence.
It has no foundation or roots.
This heart-essence of the truth
Has no body of any kind that can be shown.
The Buddhas,

However,
Open up when they see this:
Their own heart.

All the elements are perfected
Within the dominion of the sky.
All the Dharmas are perfected
In the space of the circle.[8]
All the Buddhas are perfected
In their own hearts.

This is the view of the magnificent garuda.
Everything is perfected in the heart of excellence
That does not pass into nirvana.
This is why it is called:
"The Great Perfection."

The apparition of good things that come from this
Is an obstruction.
It is grounds for error.
Essentially, they are not spoken of anywhere.

Those who do not see this total perfection
Cannot possibly see the Victorious One.

Then Vajradhara asked the Blessed One:

What is there to think about this heart-essence of perfection?

Then the Blessed One entered the equanimity of the samadhi of
the Great Compassionate One, and intentionally spoke on this specific
topic:

This heart-essence of just what is
Is not a thought,
Is not our attention,
Is not to be meditated on,
And is not a visualization.
There is nothing to visualize.

---

[8] Thig le, Bindhu

We will not be healed
By holding on,
So we let things settle into their own true natures.
Our thoughts are ideas,
So we do not think of anything at all.
The best thought
Is not to practice any philosophical theories.

We place ourselves into the fullness,
Without dividing our senses from their objects.
We must not force our senses
Into things that are not their objects,
For they do not end with these objects.
From the beginning,
This is how it is.

It is best not to divide objects as they are
From reality as it is.
In the spacious sky of the All Good
Everything is spontaneously perfect.

When we protect the cuckoo on festive occasions,
We succeed in our recitations and contemplations.
This is the same.

How could anyone else cleanse our own spirit?
We may sing out the scriptures,
But until we succeed at the thing we need: the Great Perfection,
There is no Great Perfection.

For this reason,
Even those who are engaged in the objectives of yoga
Do not meditate on this.
They do not seek it.
They let it rest in its own place.

Meditating on a mudra as a body
Is a ground for deviation.
Dividing cause and result into two
Is a path of delusion.

There are no two truths.
They don't even have a name.

Virtue and evil are non-dual.
It is best to do evil.

There is no object to be united with.
The apparent world is primordial Buddhahood.
It is not born and does not end.
It cannot be conceptualized
As being anything at all.

This is a concern for the Victorious Ones,
But there is no way at all
To meditate on it.
It is the space of the sky.

We settle into our own true natures,
The uncontrived reality of our natural condition.[9]

From the Tantra of Great Bliss, this is chapter two: Teaching that the Heart-Essence of the Secret Upadeśa is in Fact the Great Perfection.

---

[9] Gyi nar

THE COMPLETE PERFECTION
OF THE MANDALA
OF THE HEART OF THE SECRET UPADEŚA

Then Vajradhara asked the Blessed One:

What is it that is called a "view"?

The Blessed One entered the equanimity of the samadhi that has nothing to visualize, and intentionally spoke on this topic:

No one can discover
The true space of a view.

The dhyāna meditation on emptiness
Is a view,
And it fails.

Those of the vase of wisdom
Have no path.
Conceptual constructions are demons!
They are Vajradhara himself!
We are like giant garudas
Playing on the waves of the sky,
Yet there is a great difference.

This is the level of the excellence
Of wisdom that does not turn back.

It is a pure level.
This cave of wisdom
Is a resort for all of us to visit.

The spacious path is not to be stuck.
Being without a station and without ideas,
It does not depend on anything.
It does not stay anywhere.

The great Vajradhara then asked:

What is it that is called: "The equanimity of supreme pleasure"?

The Blessed One, the All Good One, entered the equanimity of the
samadhi of great bliss, and intentionally spoke on this topic:

For everyone,
The true embodiment of our bodies
Dwells forever in the pleasure that is the supreme secret.
This is the self-originating Blessed One.
It is single,
And embodiment of the highest greatness.
It is the spirit of excellence for everyone,
No one excepted.
It is the evenness of total unity.
It is pure.
We grip the halter of essential reality.
We have no desire.
We are also not free from desire,
For we join together with all the Buddhas,
None excepted.

We also do not visualize any middle way.
Totally perfect non-duality
Is the best vehicle.
It is the great bliss of all the Buddhas.
It is the true master of all the Buddhas.
It dwells within eternity itself.

Its bodies are like
The reflections of the moon.
A variety of practices for enlightenment is best.

Those present include Victorious Over Demons,
Embodiment of Totality,
Every Vehicle,
The Unmoving One,
And the rest of the ones who abide on the spokes.
Their mudras of amazing magical illusion
Include jewels, swords, lotuses,
Vajra *gandhe* drums, wheels,
Lilies and perfume flowers,
The smell of oil lamps,
Blazing tambourines and mirrors.

A great assortment of these
Appears from out of the wheel.
This is how it is:

Desire and freedom from desire,
The three worlds,
The three realms,
The three times,
The three existences,
The three excellences,
Total freedom and lack of freedom,
Equality and inequality,
And all the rest:
They spin around in the way of wheels.

All the many kinds of different mandalas,
Beyond our imagination,
And all the living beings there are,
None excepted,
And all the supreme victors,
Holy ones who have no equal,
Those of the dominion of the Dharma,
Are joined into unity
With all the Buddhas.

Vajrasattva is the Tathagata.
The Bodhicitta is, in fact, a vajra.
It is the true soul of all the Buddhas.
All of the Buddha's mandalas
Are perfected in the mandala of our supreme hero.

Vajrasattva's magnificent sky,[10]
The All Good spaciousness
Of the dominion of the Dharma,
Is a magnificent path of purity.
It liberates everyone.
It is unborn and does not end.
So we do not contemplate anything.

From the Tantra of Great Bliss, this is chapter three: The Complete Perfection of the Mandala of the Heart of the Secret Upadeśa.

---

[10] This is the first verse in chapter 30 of the Kun byed rgyal po.

TEACHING
THAT THE HEART ESSENCE
OF THE SECRET UPADEŚA
IS A ROAD THAT IS DISTANT
FOR THE TIRTHAKARAS AND THE AUDITORS

Then Vajradhara asked:

Blessed One,
Please make use of the magnificent methods of heroes
As applications for the assortment of gods.

The All Good One entered the equanimity of the samadhi where everything is an application for this assortment, and said these words:

In all the rituals made of ideas
We use a variety of rites
To bring things into union.

An awareness of our own power
Arises within us.
There is no assortment of Dharmas
That come from anyone else.

Sentient beings have conceptual boundaries
That are vast beyond thinking.
The perfectly pure Buddha
May manifest as anyone at all.

The sky appears to us
As if it were somewhere else.
The subject creates the object, everywhere.

These are not the statements
Of the children of the Victorious One.
They were put together on the side.
They deviate,
Due to our not interacting with the lives of others.

We use an atom's significance,
To posit that there is oil,
Using the reasoning
That accumulations of atoms exist in lumps,
But accumulations and atoms are incompatible,
So this has no meaning.

Dependent connections, illusion, and all the rest,
Have no methods for coupling.
They lack wisdom.

The best thing about a variety of gods
Is that they fully bring the three worlds into an essence.
Our protector is joined together
With all the Buddhas.
Through his unobstructed purity
The unsought mandala is spontaneously perfected.

The mandala of dependent origination
Is just a designation.
The virtues of purity are most vast.

We will not be satisfied with looking at a mere body.
Seeing by looking at things is not fitting.
This, therefore, is a profundity
That is greater than great.

Self-originating wisdom
Is not something to be sought out.
The path of liberation
Is also taught after liberation.

From the Tantra of Great Bliss, this is chapter four: Teaching that the Heart Essence of the Secret Upadeśa is a Far Road from the Tirthakaras and the Auditors.

TEACHING
THAT THE CONVENTIONALITIES
FOR THE INDIVIDUAL FAMILIES
OF THE SECRET UPADEŚA
ARE SUBSUMED WITHIN THE FAMILY
OF THE UNCHANGING

Then the Blessed One, the All Good One, entered the equanimity of the samadhi that shows the mandala of a hero, and intentionally made this speech:

The secret circle is not a duality.
It is the mother of pure wisdom.
She is the true Blessed One herself,
The god of the gods.
I bow to this great hero!

Sentient beings are not complicated.
The unborn is a brilliant application
For what has happened
And what will happen.
We reject the exaggerations
Of being born or not being born.

The source of all the jewels,
Forever considered to be most excellent,
Emits light.

We plant a blazing victory banner,
That is like the sky,
And the light-bearing sun
Grants us empowerment.

The pleasure of the Dharma
Is to bring forth purity.
A red lotus that is fully open
Is the best.
Desire itself is the supreme secret.

The ambrosial body of the illuminator of all things
Transforms everything,
While retaining its lordship.

We show our fist,
In the way of the Tathagata.
The wisdom of the many things
Has many kinds of greatness.
Great works of virtue
Appear to be special.

We hold to the supremacy
Of the circle that is the origin of all things.
How could anything exaggerate this heart-essence,
Which has no origin and is not born?

There has been nothing to do,
From the beginning.
This is beyond our works.

Families and wisdoms are conventionalities.
This is why the magnificent originator[11]
Is the Blessed One.

From the Tantra of Great Bliss, this is chapter five: Teaching that the Conventionalities for the Individual Families of the Secret Upadeśa are Subsumed within the Family of the Unchanging.

---

[11] 'Byung ba chen po

TEACHING ALL THE SAMAYA
FOR THE SECRET UPADEŚA

Then the Blessed One entered the equanimity of the samadhi of magnificent protection, and intentionally spoke on this topic:

The samaya themselves,
The practices,
The hosts of gods,
Their primordial good works,
Obstructions,
The development of a residence,
The five major implements,
And the five emotional problems:
These are the samaya for magnificent methods.

The branch samaya
Are fifty-two or ten.

Not to give up our guru,
To serve our guru,
Not to break the current of the mantra and the mudra,
To delight in engaging in the most pure path,
And not to speak of things that are secret:
There are fifty-two branch samaya,
But each of these fifty-two
Is split up by the wise,
Two by two,
For a sum of ten.

The five root samaya
Also have wisdoms and powers,
So there are ten,
And each of them,
Three by three,
Is also made clear,
Without distortion.

The precious jewel of samaya
Forms the vajra
That is the foundation of the ocean.

The emptiness in our stomachs is filled.
The great originator,
The Blessed One,
Dwells in fullness.
So it is that the Blessed One dwells naturally
In all living things.

We may make attributions about it,
Through our own revertedness,
But, to be brief,
Holy ones will not get self-originating liberation
From anything else.

From the Tantra of Great Bliss, this is chapter six: Teaching All the
Samaya for the Secret Upadeśa.

PRACTICING THE UNSURPASSED VEHICLE
OF THE SECRET UPADEŚA

Then the Blessed One entered the equanimity of the samadhi that is not teeming with problems, and intentionally spoke on this topic:

It is not appropriate to measure or obstruct
The body of the Sugata,
The Victorious One.
It is not infested with any problems.

Those who have desire, hatred, and ignorance,
Who act out of pride and jealousy,
Are, according to the supreme and unsurpassed vehicle,
The practitioners who turn out to be the best.

To cut through things with no regard for these five
Is the very best.
There is nothing better.

It is proclaimed that those of bad castes,
Fishermen,
People with moles,
Those with the reverted views of the inferior vehicles,
The rude,
And such people as the purple-reeded ones,[12]
Who work for the sake of killing

---

[12] sMug sbugs pa

Will succeed with this supreme vehicle.

Those who have done the five inexpiables,
Those for whom nothing is holy,
Robbers, market thieves, generals of armies,
And those who turn the wheels of evil
Will succeed using this supreme vehicle,
For it is the unsurpassed great vehicle.

Those who enjoy taking lives,
Adulterers,
Takers of what others have not given,
And those who are constantly practicing their lust
Are the recommended recipients
For this unsurpassed vehicle.

Those who practice union with mothers and sisters,
Those who eat feces and urine for their food,
Those who fight with and blame
The monks and their dhyāna meditations,
And those who burn temples and the Sutras:
These are the ones that please the Buddha.
They also act to retain the holy Dharma.
These fortunate people
Are not different than the most pure Buddha.
They play in their completion
Of the two great accumulations.

A butcher carries a sharp razor.
Those who work for purity
In the abodes of the six kinds of living beings
Are heroes on the road to freedom.
They embody enlightenment.

The land that all the Buddhas go to
Is happy.
Equanimity without thoughts
Is the embodiment of the Dharma.
We are not held by what we take in,
Like the moon on the water.
Through the playfulness of the All Good One
The profundities of the vowels and consonants are taught.

E Ma'o!
The meaning of the Dharma has emerged!
The practices of a master of the Dharma are pure.

Without regard to cleanliness and filth
We eat everything.
Being without compassion,
We kill everything.
When we unite with the things we see
This is what is called: "The Supreme Vehicle."

From the Tantra of Great Bliss, this is chapter seven: Practicing the Unsurpassed Vehicle of Secret Upadeśa.

OFFERING WITHOUT CONCEPTIONS:
IF WE OURSELVES OFFER THE SECRET UPADEŚA TO OURSELVES
WE WILL HAVE MADE OFFERINGS TO ALL THE MANDALAS

Then the Blessed One, the glorious All Good One, entered the equanimity of the samadhi in which we are kings when we offer bodily fluids and excrement to all the mandalas, and intentionally he spoke on this topic:

We must not use the smell of sandalwood
For our offerings to the mandalas of the three jewels,
And to the three existences.
We must use the five objects of desire
For our offerings.

Know that there is no mandala
Other than the self.[13]
Our true self is the owner of the mandala.
Feces are implements for our success at equanimity.
To eat them physically,
And to make offerings of them
Will please everyone in all the castes.
The goddesses will also be satisfied.

---

[13] bDag, Atman

In his effort to see Bodhisattvas,
A skillful person who has a vessel,
Whether it is a new vessel
Or an old vessel
It is not definite,
Fills it full with feces, urine, unclean bodily fluids, and blood,
And makes offerings with it
Every day and every night
To the great mandala of his true self.

Once the mandala of the primary deity is pleased,
He will succeed with all the mandalas
Of all the family lineages,
With no exceptions.
He will see the mandala
Of the unsurpassed.

When we make offerings with a new vase
By generating, beaming out, reconvening,
Display and illumination
Of a mandala that measures a hundred hundred-thousand miles,
These beautiful offerings we make will not be blessed,
And will not be enjoyed.
They will not cause our siddhis to actually appear.

Those who are wise in methods
Make offerings to themselves.
There is a difference between
The offering of a hundred hundred-thousand mandalas
And the mandala that we offer to ourselves,
For it is a great siddhi that lets us accomplish everything,
While we take on the attitude
Of a great lord of wrath,
Whose costume is a mandala of angry frowns.

Then even though the written letters may be evident to us,
We do not see the mandala of the peaceful ones.

From the Tantra of Great Bliss, this is chapter eight: Offering without
Conceptions: If We Ourselves Offer the Secret Upadeśa to Ourselves We
Will Have Made Offerings to All the Mandalas.

TEACHING
THE NATURES OF THE FIVE GREAT MANDALAS
TO BE OUR FIVE EMOTIONAL PROBLEMS
IN THEIR PURITY

Then the Blessed One entered the equanimity of the samadhi of the uniqueness of the holy truth, and intentionally spoke on this topic:

Then the king who holds the secrets
Made a request to the Blessed One
So that the meaning of these secrets
Might be retained.
He said: "Please explain what is holy."

So the holy lord,
Who is the soul of all things,[14]
Meditated on three distinct mandalas
Which the Buddhas who appear throughout the three times
Practice in their bodies, speech, and minds.

On a vajra ground that is unchanging and stable,
Resting in the center of the dominion of the sky,
We are equal as one with unsurpassed wisdom.

Practitioners who are doing the practice
Of the path to wisdom's freedom
Are killing all the sentient beings.

---

[14] Kun bdag

They are shaking up the three worlds,
And when everyone has been killed,
They will be in the land of the unshaking Buddha,
Whose vajra body
Is the king of this supreme family.[15]
His very essence is clean,
And has no stain.

The undammed river of Buddhahood
Is a great blessing
For those who work on the practice
Of the total perfection of enlightenment.

When we meditate brilliantly
On the mandala of ignorance,
This is the mandala of a Tathagata.
It is the completion of all the mandalas of the families.

The mandalas of anger, pride, lust,
Jealousy, and all the rest,
Are perfected in the mandala of the Victorious One.

If we desire empowerment
Into these five holy mandalas,
We will be empowered.

Vision keepers[16] desire supreme Buddhahood.
The mandalas of the five come from it,
And all of these are what we truly work with.
These mandalas,
Beginning with lust,
Are undivided in body, speech, and mind,
And are pure in the samayas for the families.

The king of secret mantras,
Vajradhara,
Comes from the wisdom of selflessness.
Those who are working on the meaning
Of the secret vajra
Must work with all the Buddhas.

---

[15] Rigs
[16] Rig 'dzin

To do this,
We meditate on these secret mandalas.

One who worships the Three Jewels,
Performing services for the mandalas of these five,
Will succeed in the three excellences.
His heart will be stable.
He will attain wisdom.

Practitioners who practice mantras for these mandalas,
Who have inferior intellects,
Who have an attitude of reverted views,
Who eat vomit and reject the Buddha,
And who are experts in the meanings of the views,
Are supreme practitioners in the practice of mantra.
They move after the totality of the sky,
For all the mandalas of the Dharma
Are subsumed within the mandala of the sky.
So it is that without offering up any mandalas
We have the great mandala of primordial Buddhahood.

A yogin who practices this is fortunate.
He plays in the spontaneously-formed objects of illusion,
Without separating his own objectives
From those of others.

The self-originating mandala
Is perfected within ourselves.
The character of the sky
Neither acquires nor discards anything.

The teachings on the mandala of ignorance,
As it plays in the illusions of relative reality,
And emerges from the mandala of non-conceptualization,
Are amazing.

From the Tantra of Great Bliss this is chapter nine of the Vajra Reality
of the Ultimate Truth of the Secret Upadeśa: Teaching the Natures of the
Five Great Mandalas to Be Our Five Emotional Problems in Their Purity.

THE SECRET UPADEŚA
ON ACHIEVING
BOTH SIDDHIS WITH SIGNS
AND SIDDHIS WITHOUT SIGNS

Then the Blessed One, the All Good One, entered the equanimity of the samadhi that subsumes the siddhis, and he intentionally spoke on this topic:

The mandalas of body, speech, and mind
Are miraculous.
The heart-essence of supreme siddhi
Is the Blessed One,
The body of a *Nṛi*.[17]

The king of the ashes of *Nṛi*,
Vajradhara,
Has brought together all the heart-essences
Of the secret mantra.
He does not reject the five kinds of living beings.
He retains the four Maras.

We do not visualize that our bodies, speech, or minds
Are truly in their own place.
The equanimity that does not dwell on anything
Is that our body, speech, and mind
Are a vajra embodiment.

---

[17] This is the seed syllable of the word for "human."

The realms of sentient beings are endless.
It is difficult for a Victorious One to find Buddhahood.
This is why the mandalas abide
In the center of the pure dominion of the sky,
And are all subsumed into a Hūṃ.

We meditate that our *citta*[18] is a Hūṃ.
We brilliantly put our own form into this Hūṃ.
The mandala of Hūṃ
Is a magnificent light.
We contemplate on its manifestation
As the five colors,
Vajrasattva being the primary of the Victorious Ones.

Our *citta* is a Hūṃ,
Then, suddenly,
Our body, speech, and mind
Are Vajradhara.

The primacy of Hūṃ
Is the supremacy of our lord,
The heart-essence of the embodiment
Of all the mandalas of all the families.
They are condensed into a Hūṃ.

This Hūṃ is the supreme syllable.
It is a light that blazes
At the center of the heaps that form us.

It shatters,
And a five pointed vajra shines forth.
It is the vajra of the heart-essence of the Victorious Ones.
It is the supreme vajra.
It is Vajradhara.

The heart-essence of this vajra is stable.
It subsumes the wheel,
And all the rest.
A mandala that resembles a Hūṃ
Is an astonishing miracle.

---

[18] The Sanskrit word for "mind."

It shatters,
And there is the path to the Buddha's enlightenment.

This is a vast accomplishment.
To attain the siddhi
Of secretly joining into union
With the Buddhas of the past, future, present,
And those whose appearance is undefined,
There is no other way
Than the shattering of syllables.
Even if the Victorious Ones looked for one,
They would not find it.

There is no other significance to having siddhis
Than this.
One who has perfection,
Who is skilled in the applications of the senses,
Will not consider melting all their senses together.

When the Hūṃ in a picture or a drawing
Is illuminated,
We do not become attached to Vajradhara,
And we are not attached to any attachment.
This is the supreme attachment.
It is the king.

When we do not visualize any entities,
We fully complete all the retreats.
It is difficult to find the siddhi of greatness.
We will succeed when we rely on wisdom as a method.

Mere names seem to depend on other things,
But directly perceived happiness
Comes from ourselves.

From the Tantra of Great Bliss, this is chapter ten: The Secret Upadeśa
on Achieving Both Siddhis With Signs and Siddhis Without Signs.

NOT CLAIMING
THAT THERE IS A TEACHING THAT SAYS:
"THE SECRET UPADEŚA ARE SOMETHING
OF SOME SORT
THAT WE MEDITATE ON."

Then the Blessed One entered the equanimity of the samadhi in which there is nothing to meditate on, and intentionally spoke on this topic:

Those who would attain the Buddha's enlightenment
Must look into the meaning of the Unwritten.
We must investigate the speech that has no essence.
The excellent way of enlightenment is a great happiness.

Manifestations of the vajra of wisdom
Do not divide Buddhahood into a cause and a result,
For we have come forth from out of the Dharma of the Unwritten.
For this reason,
People who are true manifestations
Do not display any definite physical accoutrements,
For we do not take measure of the meaning
Of something that is invisible.

The holiness of the wheel of the Dharma
Is that it is not visible
In the same way that the conceptualized deeds of a manifestation are.
The supreme embodiment of this heart-essence
Has been made famous in the Tantra of the Unwritten.[19]

The hearts of all the Buddhas,
And likewise of all the vajra teachers,
Are endowed with the five wisdoms.
This is the heart of hearts.

A heart of secrets is sure,
Yet it becomes a path toward every fruition.
The vajra of wisdom is like the sky.

Without visualizing anything at all,
There is stupidity.
All the Buddhas of the four times,
With no exceptions,
May seek for this,
Over three eons,
But even these Buddhas will not see it.

When physical beings
Who have bodies, speech, and minds,
See what is invisible,
They will have completed the third level,
But even Bodhisattvas on the tenth level
Retain the finest samaya
For the Buddha's supernatural perception.

In the center of what seems to be the sky,
Without any visualization,
There is the holiness of the Buddha's mandala.
It is not to be visualized,
But once we find it,
We are mature.

The contemplation of the Buddhas and Bodhisattvas
Is an unchanging equanimity.
We do not meditate on any heart-spell for any mantra.
We do not cling
To the offering of a mudra.

---

[19] Ye ge med pa'i rgyud. It is possible, but not certain, that this refers to a text by the same title that I have translated and is to be found in Secret Sky: The Ancient Tantras on Vajrasattva's Magnificent Sky.

When we are not attached to writing implements,
Our stainless protectors are the Three Jewels,
A thought that brings us into true dhyāna meditation
Is made manifest as the five wisdoms,
And other holy things.

The Buddhas are equal to the dominion of the sky.
We meditate while in a place of supreme Buddhahood,
With mudras that include cast images.
We dwell on the path of total freedom.
Using it as a basis,
We find the path of the Victorious One,
And then stay within the essence
Of the mudra of totality.

The immeasurable palace of blazing wisdom
Is possessed of a throne and of offerings.
In the heart-essence of self-aware equanimity,
We are primordially perfect.

We abide in the essence.
The essence of a heart of equanimity
Is not something that there are any teachings about,
We do not, however, dwell on causes
That come from anything else.
We dwell within the true purity of a mirror.

The heart-essence
Of the three total unions[20]
Is not something that can be exemplified.

The path of the Victorious One
Is the magnificent mandala
Of the vajra sky.
We do not work on any heart spell,
Such as the Vajra Wheel.
We give up exaggerations.

Within a circle,
We settle smoothly into an equanimity without visualizations.
This resembles the pure worship of the Buddha.

---

[20] Kun spyor gsum

Without seeking it,
We settle into an invisible reality.
This is meditation.

When we look around for this and that,
We will not get the meaning of this coming from that.
Perfectly pure Buddhahood
Turns into a long road.

Being without attachment to any true meaning,
Either internal or external,
We do not settle on anything.
One who quits doing this
Has the supreme path of freedom.
One who meditates
On the three vajra indivisibilities
Is joined into
Vajrasattva himself.

When we touch on this,
We stay with it,
In the same way that alligators do not let people go.

From the Tantra of Great Bliss, this is chapter eleven: Not Saying That
There is a Teaching that Says: "The Secret Upadeśa Are Something of
Some Sort That We Meditate On."

TEACHING
THAT THE SECRET UPADEŚA
ARE BEYOND THE LEVEL OF PERFECTION
AND THAT THERE IS NOTHING TO LEARN
ON THE LEVELS

Then the Blessed One entered the equanimity of the samadhi of not studying, and intentionally spoke on this topic:

A Bodhisattva is an embodiment of a vajra.
He spins the wheel of the orations brilliantly.
The embodiment of the three bodies
Is A.

Not to be divided by anything whatsoever
Is the embodiment of a vajra.
In the end,
We give up our differences.
When something transcends sounds, names, and words,
It will demonstrate no personal essence.

Those who have achieved the level of being fearless heroes
Do not need to study about the level of Buddhahood.
It is insubstantial.
It is pure by its very nature.
The Vajrayana is unsurpassed!

A teaching that there are entities

Within these Dharmas that are unborn
Has not been proclaimed.
The Victorious Ones have taught about generation.

E Ma'o!
Dharmas are like dreams.
Appearance is empty.
It is secluded by its very nature.
The supreme level of unsurpassed wisdom
Is not to dwell on the levels of the Bodhisattvas.

If excellent practitioners
Who practice mantras
Wish to discover the unshaking supreme Dharma,
They must be taught everything about desire,
And when they practice their desires
With the wisdom of lust
They will have studied through the levels,
And have reached to the end.

This luminous bliss is like a water-moon.
There is just an appearance.
There is nothing that is naturally there.
We may have achieved the level of the Buddha's purification,
But we will succeed by using the teachings
On the good things about desire.

With no attachment to form,
We will be free from attachment,
Then there will be the cohesion of the first five.

It has been proclaimed
That the levels themselves are not to be studied.
For as many eons as the sands of the Ganges,
Inconceivable numbers of living beings
Have worked in fields,
And for applications that will succeed.

Yogins who are masters at mantras
Meditate on supreme enlightenment,
Then, all of a sudden,

They kill everything.
After that,
They are born as the children
Of the one who is victorious over the Victorious Ones.

When the conventionalities of relative reality are absent,
The ultimate reality of perfect enlightenment
May appear or not appear.
When we do not seek it,
Everything will be at peace,
For there is no true nature.

We are free of things like illusions and optical deceptions.
We leave behind the levels where we count ideas.
The embodiment of equanimity
Does not divide cause and result.
It is like a water-moon,
Or a dream,
Or something like that.

Everything is clear in just this self-awareness,
So we say: "This self-awareness is also like this!"
This is not something that we teach to someone else.
This is why we settle our self-awareness,
Which is self-originating,
Into its own peace.

This is beyond the dominion of the non-conceptual.
That is why the heart-essence of equanimity
Is like a water-moon.

Do not separate the body from the wisdom.
The heart that does not waver,
And does not visualize anything at all,
Transcends the word "water-moon."

It is beyond thought,
And transcends the things we work toward.
It is totally lacking in verbal conventionalities.
We have no object for our visualization
That is called: "Meditation,"
We do not give it the name of a transmission,
So we are not confused by any other concern of logic.

This is single,
Primordially vast,
And primordially present,
So all the Buddhas are also stamped with its seal.

The true character of the All Good One
Is to play around in playfulness.
From the beginning,
The All Good One
Is the level of everyone!

Its greatness and smallness,
Its vastness and dimensions,
Are not to be measured.

The basis for both stability and shaking
Is not present without attachment,
And without thought,
So we must not remain attached
To the flavors of samadhi.

Our clinging to entities
Is primordially cleansed,
So we do not have even a name
For what is not an entity.
For this reason,
This supremely secret reality
Will not be heard of elsewhere,
With the organ of the ear.

In the same way,
The organ of the tongue as well
Has not even an atom to say about it.
This is beyond conventional objects,
And there is no part of it that is merely dedication.

There is nothing to show
By saying: "This."

From the Tantra of Great Bliss, this is chapter twelve: Teaching that the Secret Upadeśa are Beyond the Level of Perfection and that There is Nothing to Learn on the Levels.

SHOWING
THE DEVIATION THERE IS
IN DIVIDING RETREAT PRACTICE
FOR THE SECRET UPADEŚA
INTO FOUR TYPES

The Victorious One who holds a vajra in his hand[21]
Asked all the great heroes
About the four kinds[22] of retreat.

So the Blessed One, the All Good One, entered the equanimity of the
samadhi of the retreat, and intentionally spoke on this topic:

The mandalas of the body
Are as any as the sands.
The number of them for the speech and the mind
Is just the same.
When we are truly working on the mandala of the Buddha,
As demonstrated through our five supernatural cognitions,
We brilliantly organize the domain of the world,
Using our vajra body, speech, and mind.

Everything is the body of Vajrasattva.
This is inconceivable.
We make a place,

---

[21] Lag na rdo rje 'chang
[22] bsNyen pa rnam gzhi. Page 475.2. "gZhi" here is a mistake for "bZhi," as
clarified by the colophon on 478.6.

And a spontaneously made mandala blazes forth there.

Our true selves are embodiments of the Bodhicitta.
So it is that Vairochana and the rest
Blaze forth as embodiments of Vajrasattva.
In the same way,
Our embodiment of the Bodhicitta,
May blaze in any way at all,
But our true self
Does not move away from enlightenment.

Vajrasattva and the others who are Bodhisattvas
Did this retreat.
It is called: "The supreme retreat."

Those who are the finest of the true practitioners
May inspect the generative forces and domains
Of the vajra heaps,
But according to the Vajrasattva from the Ganges,[23]
The embodiment of the Bodhicitta's true soul
Is what we call our true retreat.
The lord of the mantras has spoken brilliantly on this.

In our efforts to work on this mandala,
We use the heart-essence of our awareness
To meditate on a body.
It blazes with Oṃ Ā: Hūṃ Traṃ Sva

An isolated essence of appearance and emptiness
Is also the best thing to work on.
A lord of mantras who meditates
Invokes this heart-spell
When doing his practice.

Any mandala at all will be fine.
The word that makes something a magnificent practice
Is the heart-spell that is our Yidam deity's own mantra.
When we chant it we are Vajradhara.

We think of the five Vajrasattvas,
Who can surely be embodied

---

[23] Gangā'i rdo rje'i sems dpa'

In any way that pleases them,
As if they were ornaments for our crown.
These masters succeeded in achieving the wisdom vajra
Through using secret mantras.

Those who keep their lord on their head,
Live in an elevated mood,
For they are in the visible presence of Vajrasattva.

So it is that we arrange the deities
For a retreat that is in the sky.

The master from the path of the vajra,
In the mandala of the lotus of the sky,
Swirls the master's ambrosia
Into the lotus.

The body of a lusty woman or a naga woman
May be most certainly amazing,
But it is blessed by the great wisdom of purity,
So we must meditate on it.
It will bring our retreat practice to a great completion.

Those who know the applications for the retreat samaya
Will have a quick retreat.
A quick retreat
Is one where once we know that a meditation,
Such as Vajrasattva,
Will, of its own nature,
Shine out as a magnificent practice,
Then we will know how to cleanse
A thousand hundred-thousands
Of mandalas of blazing light,
Circles of luminescence,
Into the Bodhicitta.

Through a summary understanding of this essence,
We will know the samaya for the retreat.
This is also the best way to do a retreat.
It is the basis for what we have to work on.

We must unite in a magnificent project.
A is the mandala for the retreat.

Oṃ is the close retreat.
Hūṃ is called: "The project."
Sva is proclaimed to be a magnificent project.
Hūṃ is the master who sits on our heads.

If there were any source or application
That would make us go in an instant
To the excellent abode of Amitabha,
Then it would also be fitting
That we seize the Buddha in our hands.

The samaya for the retreat of the Buddha
Are for the children of the Victorious One
Who understand union.
We join up on the level of unsurpassed wisdom,
In only a moment.

This approach to Buddhahood
Uses our awareness.
Buddhahood and awareness are inseparable.
They are together on the level of the unsurpassed.
The words of the mantra are a holy project.
It is a magnificent project.

Now the four kinds of retreat practice
Must each be subdivided into four parts.
The mandala of total purity
Has no divisions,
So it is the best approach.

It is the rapid retreat,
For we are perfected spontaneously.
We apply everything to our practice.
The best way to work on things
Is without acquiring or abandoning anything.
This is not a place to stay
For practitioners of severe austerities.
Those who retain the A and the Par[24]
Wish for some illusory happiness to appear,

---

[24] It is likely that these syllables indicate nerve channels, in keeping with the descriptions found in The Tantra on Vajrasattva's Magnificent Sky. See p. 221 of Secret Sky: The Ancient Tantras on Vajrasattva's Magnificent Sky.

But this has the problem
That we are clinging.

There is one true nature,
But it is not certain how we will see it,
And how it will appear to us.

The happiness there is in our desire for appearances
In our seeking attitude,
And in mandalas such as the retreat practice
Is one where this obstructs that,
And there are major problems.

Enlightenment is a portal for every avenue.
Meditating on apparel is like a moon on the water.
Without attachments,
And without stain,
Things will happen.
To meditate on them
Is a childish occupation.

From the Tantra of Great Bliss, this is chapter thirteen: Showing the Deviation There Is in Dividing Retreat Practice for the Secret Upadeśa into Four Types.

TEACHING
THAT THE SECRET UPADEŚA DO NOT DWELL
WITHIN THE VIEWS
OF THE SAUTRĀNTIKAS AND THEIR KIND

Then the Blessed One, the All Good One, entered the equanimity of the samadhi that is not static, and spoke intentionally on this topic:

Neither samsara nor nirvana
Thinks of anything at all,
Or exists anywhere.

Yoga is rapid.
When we engage in it
We will not think about any non-conceptualization,
But we will use the wisdom that understands specifics
As a true objective of holiness,
A path of truth.

This is beyond the topics we talk and think about.
We use the essence of our self-awareness,
Whether or not it comes from causes and conditions,
To bring things into equanimity.

This is the basis for the true essence of all things.
The ten perfections are a single wisdom.
To assume that things that exist
Come from out of a non-existence,
Or that habitual patterns on the surface,

Such as illusions and dreams,
Are like clouds,
Or to assume that non-existence
Comes out of existence,
Where the wisdom of peace
Is a deep depression,
And we live in our attachments
To the flavors of samadhi,
Then we will fall into the cessation
Preferred by the Auditors.

An attitude in which we think:
"I am meditating"
Occurs,
Then, in a peaceful abiding on unexaggerated emptiness,
We have an unceasing absence of consciousness.
Our minds do not think about any conceptualizations.
We simply get rid of our ordinary consciousness.
Our fears and our understandings are not joined together.

After we have personally appeared
On the level of the heart-essence of wisdom
For a long time,
It is fitting that we succeed.
If we throw our minds
Onto the trails of events and feelings,
Or become attached to the flavors of samadhi,
Then we have not cleared away
The extreme positions
Of the two horns
Of eternalism and nihilism.

This ordinary mind is a naughty boy,
Born into a crowd that has no consciousness.
We do not dwell on our mind's hopes and fears,
But meditate on something that is pure,
Something that we do not visualize.

We rest in equanimity,
Without thinking of anything at all,
Without visualizing,
And without contriving anything.
We do not have the attitude

That holds to things as being merely atoms,
For this is also the holy dominion of the Dharma.
It is the wind of unborn and uncontrived wisdom.

The omniscient king of wisdom
Keeps count of the finest hearts
Who plummet the depths
Of the three times,
The three embodiments,
The three excellences,
And the wisdom *bhaga*.

This is visible,
And it is appropriate to think about it.
A demarcated consciousness does not occur
In any of the definitions we make with false ideas.

When we are not distracted
From being focused one-pointedly on our objectives,
We are level in our parts,
Totally even,
Equal in our fields.
The way of peaceful abiding is to be found in this.

We understand that
The true nature of a multifaceted entourage
Is not singular or plural.

Without a one,
There will not be a many.
If we say that the many are in the one,
The two horns of eternalism and nihilism become evident.
For this reason,
We assemble a text about the two truths,
Then we finish up with all the established theoretics,
Using the essential reality of each individual one,
As we hold onto our own established conclusions.
We believe that dharmas are illusory.

Those who wear the rosary of wisdom have everything.
They dwell on the levels of the Perfections,
But the meaning of this is unthinkable.
Even the Victorious Ones have not thought about it.

For this reason,
The dhyāna[25] of greatest virtue
Is just dhyāna.
It is not something to think about.

This is a reality we do not think about
And do not study.
Wisdom is born out of our own ideas.
We give the name of a gate
To a narrow place,
And use our minds
To seek clarity in isolation.
We take a remoteness in our spirits
To be isolation.
When we analyze this,
We will be using this analysis for our meditations.
We give it the names of cause and result,
And carefully discriminate both virtue and vice.
We say: "I have appeared into this world!"
We develop a supreme joy in taking things up and casting them off.

Furthermore,
An embodiment of unsurpassed enlightenment
Transcends names, words, and dhyāna,
Which are a long road to perfect Buddhahood.
We must not remain on it.

A mere name takes on the power of a word.
This does not happen after the fashion of mantras.
This Dharma is unborn.
There is something special about its true essence.
From out of something that we do not visualize,
And we do not conceptualize,
The Buddha of wisdom brilliantly appears.

The Buddha did not appear.
There is also no Dharma.
The Sangha did not happen,
And will not be formed.

---

[25] Tibetan: bSam gtan. Chinese: Ch'an. Japanese: Zen

Attachment and non-attachment
Are pathways for words.
According to the middle way,
They are like the echoes from the rocks.

It is said that bliss and sorrow have the same cause.
The protector of those who live
Speaks with his mind.

From the Tantra of Great Bliss, this is chapter fourteen: Teaching that the Secret Upadeśa do not Dwell within the Views of the Sautrāntikas and Their Kind.

THE SECRET UPADEŚA ON HOW LIBERATION THROUGH THE THREE YOGAS IS UNSTAINED BY FAULTS

Then the Blessed One, the glorious All Good One, entered the equanimity of the samadhi where everyone is liberated from levels, and he intentionally spoke on this topic:

The supreme and the supremely humble
Are fields for deliverance.
Those who do not take the vase of empowerment to their ears,
Who reject the unsurpassed,
Who ridicule their gurus,
And do such things,
Are fields for deliverance.

We meditate on being embodied
As a keeper of secret mantras.
We contemplate that there are five seed-syllables
On spokes that are at our navel.
On the five peaks of our two hands,
There is a sun to the right,
And a moon to the left.

There are ten thrones,
Ornamented with precious jewels,
For the male and female great ones of the five lineages.
The five fathers are to the right.
The five mothers are to the left.

We set out the scripture
For the letters of the seed syllables
And the mantra.
We recite them,
And our bodies transform into blazing light.

In the place of the previous entity,
There is a moon.
We rest on top of it,
Laying on our backs.

There is a moon in our hearts.
We imagine that on top of it
There is the body of the Remover of Obstructions.[26]

We recite his heart-spell,[27]
Then join our hands,
And from the juncture where they join,
Clouds of joy pour out.

The body of the Remover of Obstructions
Has the fathers and mothers of the five lineages
On its head.
These ten are a mandala.
It blazes with light,
And, with just a motion of a twist of our hand,
The immeasurable palace of the Remover of Obstructions
Opens up with a blast,
And a hero comes forth.

He comes forth with the full insignia
Of an embodiment of the Victorious Ones,
A light that illuminates everything blazes forth,
And we chant the heart-spells of the lineages.[28]
The two groups of five melt into ten,
Then dissolve into space.
We form into a body,
And blaze as the Remover.

---

[26] sGrib pa rnam sel
[27] sNying po
[28] Rigs

We liberate the apparent world with its three excellences,
While there is not an atom there to be liberated.
There is nothing to take up or cast off.
This is a path of freedom.

Nothing binds or frees us.
This is the dominion of the Dharma.
When self-awareness becomes completely clear,
It prevents our losing freedom
Due to killing even the most excellent of sentient beings.
We only turn into Vairochana.

Once we maintain a continuous samadhi
That all sentient beings are pure from the very beginning,
We may kill the supreme or the supremely humble,
And unite in bliss with our consort's sky.
This is not liberation.
It is supreme happiness.

When we understand that
There is nothing for compassion to take hold of
In the mandala of non-conceptual wisdom,
We liberate everyone in the three realms,
With no exceptions,
While Vajrasattva's own body
Is the equal of all things,
From the very beginning.

Sentient beings come from ideas.
Sentient beings are certainly not Buddhas.

One with the vigor of youth,
Who eats horse meat, dog meat, and ox meat,
Will surely be born into the five families of Victorious Ones.

That which is called "life"[29]
Is the sky.
In the sky,
There is just the sky.

---

[29] Srog

A person who is wise in primordial playfulness
Is a hero of magnificent methods.
For him,
There is nothing to be taken in with compassion.

The fire at the end of the eon
Will burn the sky.
The water of life will churn the ocean.
The playfulness of wisdom is also life.
The way in which a rainbow melts into the sky
Is how life itself melts into the sky.
Life and the sky are one.

This is why there are no sentient beings
To be taken in with compassion.
It has been proclaimed by Vajrasattva
That a division in the holiness of sentient beings
Does not exist.

For people who are skilled in methods,
Killing emotional problems is the supreme objective.
We fight with monks on the path to enlightenment.
The Blessed One has proclaimed
That those who are the most excellent of the Auditors,
Are the best of all.

To desire the unexcelled level of wisdom,
And enter the equanimity of the level of enlightenment
Is wonderful.
It is liberation.
It is a path of happiness,
But it is not the same as a path of freedom.
There is no supreme bliss in it.
That is why we perfect ourselves
Through doing the five inexpiables,
And dwell on the level of supreme wisdom.

We may do all the deeds of union and of emancipation,
But we will not have done even an atom's part of anything.

The sky does not give birth to ideas,
While ideas themselves are like the sky.
The unattached sky is free from attachments.

Our greatest personal objective
Appears to be the sky.
We are fully cleansed in the Bodhicitta,
Which is why great compassion does nothing at all.

The superior quality
Of this great wave of superior virtues
Is never recommended to anyone.

From the Tantra of Great Bliss, this is chapter fifteen: The Secret Upadeśa on How Liberation through the Three Yogas is Unstained by Faults.

THE SAMAYA OF UNION

Then the Blessed One, the All Good One, entered the equanimity of the samadhi in which we are liberated through union, and intentionally spoke on this topic:

Those who wish to join together
In the Mahamudra,
And attain a result of total liberation
Must take care for the path of enlightenment.
To do this they will place their mother, children, and sisters
Into the center of the circle of blessings.
On its spokes we place women of good family.
Then we meditate on the Mahamudra.

We clench our left hand at our heart,
Then draw it away from our heart,
As we would an iron hook.
Then we take hold of the white lady.[30]
We eat our own excrement,
And make a summons with the heart-spell.

Our right eye is turned up,
And our left eye is turned down.
Then, with a huge smile,
We recite Oṃ.

---

[30] dKar mo

There is an Oṃ in our secret vajra.
Its edges are encircled with *Maha*.
We imagine that there is a Muṃ
On the white lady's *bhaga*.

The tips of the two tongues meet.
The mouths join.
The blessing of the white lady
Is her magnificent dominion.
There is a secret joining
Of the two sets of sensory powers.

We recite the heart-spell,
And generate excitement.
If we then eat semen, blood, and excrement,
We will succeed in all the mandalas of the lineages,
None excepted.

All the women in the world's domain,
However, many there may be,
Use the union with a physical mudra,
And this is very practical for all of them.

The vajra rests in the center of the lotus,
Without removing it,
Resting it there like that.

Once we see that we are joined together,
Our lips join.
In this we hold numberless ten-millions of secret mantras.
All the Buddhas pour forth from this.

This is how we will attain
The enlightenment that is like a vajra sky.
This is the greatest secret of all the Buddhas.
It is a miraculous samaya.
We keep our pathway
On the goddess's own crown,
And through her blessings,
Our bodies transform,
And as we exhale, we chant: Hūṃ.

A master chants: Hūṃ,
And his body becomes a blazing Hūṃ.
The woman,
Whoever she may be,
Is a goddess,
A blessed queen of the Hūṃ.

Insert the vajra into the woman's opening,
Keeping the secret union stable.
Move and thrust.
Then make a union into non-duality,
And all the Buddhas,
None excepted,
Will emerge.

This is why it is proclaimed
That the master of the Hūṃ will succeed.

The Maṃ, Paṃ, and Traṃ are as they were from of yore.

A woman is one who has taken the way of the goddess,
And stands upon the spoke of a blazing wheel.
This woman,
Whoever she may be,
May sometimes think about the way of the path.
It has been proclaimed that she will succeed
As a master of a path such as this.

Women with young bodies are beautiful,
But we must also not discriminate.
Those who are both young and old,
Who are not beautiful,
Are blessed with the arrogance of a goddess.

The heart-spell for arrogant women and their kind is:

Hūṃ Lāsye | Traṃ Māle | Trī: Girti | Anirti |

We recite this heart spell,
As is fitting.
Our body transforms into blazing light,
And suddenly we are uniting with a beautiful youth,
Whether she is old or young,

With this as our only reality.

We do not let go.
We use the fan,
Then we eat and drink of the fluids and excrement.
We will transform into a lord,
Such as Earth Heart.[31]

We chant the heart-spell:
Dhūpusālogandhema.

There is a transformation in ways,
And she is a sixteen year old girl.
She has taken on a body worthy of worship.
We make up fantasies,
And fluids emerge from out of secret pathways.

The cave of the lotus brings pleasure.
A thrill of many delights appears there at the gate.
If we drink from and lick
Girls who we meditate to have the forms
Of beings such as Maitreya,
We will become masters of the goddesses of offering.

When we chant: Krodha Khakṣi
Women in a wrathful rage
Will surround the doors of the wheel and its spokes.
Stationed there.
We chant the heart-spells of these four wrathful women,
And contemplate their forms.
When we are actually uniting with a woman,
Our fluids will satisfy her with an array of delights.

We do not stop with fluids and excrement.
When we eat and drink them with a crone[32] or two,
We will become masters over the great wrathful one, Vijaya,
And others.

This is how the great mandala of the blazing wrathful one
Is described to be supremely magnificent.

---

[31] Sa snying
[32] Dregs mo

It is a brilliant delight
For all the groups of women and girls
In uncounted thousands of ten-millions of worlds.

We must use this lust that makes us glorious
To make ourselves stable.
The master of discipline
For this community with its women of power[33]
Has magnificent methods.

A master who would control the haughty
Recites the heart-spell,
And makes them crazy.
He unites with them playfully,
And wakes them up.

A master is one who considers all women
To be women of power,
And will actually unite with all of them.
Within the pathways of his vajra
The fluids will emerge.

He sprinkles her feet with lilies,
And pleases her so that she is satisfied,
Coming forward at the door.

When both partners are drinking and licking,
Like jackals gliding over a mountain slope,
We are masters for the women of power.
Moreover,
All the mandalas of the supreme victor
Beam out and reconvene,
And we must work accordingly.

A lord and master of all the secret mantras
Who has held all these women,
As many as there may be,
And has satisfied their lust,
Is equal to all the Victorious Ones,
And will enjoy a vajra ecstasy.

---

[33] dBang phyug ma

After we join the vowels and the consonants together,
We stamp them with a seal,
An elaborate mudra.
In the space of a single moment,
Everything is united.

The woman that is the white lady,
Women of good family,
Goddesses,
Naginis,
And all the rest
Are to be joined with.
There is no doubt.

Horses, cows, buffalo,
Dogs, pigs, vultures, bears,
And all the rest,
Whichever they may be,
Are Naginis.

Goddesses and their kind
Have things to gain and to lose,
And there are no women's organizations
That they do not join.

When it is the time to engage in a great practice
For the earth,
With its rocks and trees,
We must gather with the lords of the mandala.

The vision of self-awareness
Is the greatest of yogas,
For it clears away our ideas,
And we join with something that we do not gain or lose.

We use an attitude of having no doubt
To unite with our mothers and sisters in samaya.
We are bound by the mudras of our shared ideas.
In splendor, we unite as one together
In a glorious bliss.

Those who are expert in the union of the Mahāyoga
Turn the wheel about a land where there is happiness,

So why should we even talk about
How those who have attained the unchanging
Use a view that is stainless and pure
To promote the unexcelled pathway of the Buddha's enlightenment?

All unions are the vestiges
Of those who move in bliss.

The dakini's secret moon,
An embodiment of the circle,[34]
Is, for a Bodhisattva,
The substance of all the Buddhas.

By travelling over three paths,
Or over any path,
We will not be purified.
Critical boys do not understand union.
Through union we get unsurpassed wisdom.
This is truly it.
There is no doubt.

The three times are one.
There is no difference.
We have no past.
We have no future.
This has been present since the primordial.

In being encompassed by the embodiment of the Dharma
We are one.
This is why the great
Live with a true nature of greatness.
Nothing whatsoever divides us.
This is why the totality of union
Is the supreme bliss.

From the Secret Upadeśa of the Tantra of Great Bliss, this is chapter sixteen: The Samaya of Union.

---

[34] Thig le

THE HEART-ESSENCE OF THE SECRET UPADEŚA IS NOT STAINED BY ANY FAULT

Then the Blessed One, the All Good One, entered the equanimity of the samadhi in which we are not stained by faults, no matter what we do, and intentionally spoke on this topic:

The sorrows of living beings
Do not move within this Bodhicitta.
In this same way,
We live in an equanimity
That is like the end of the sky,
Which matches with the detailed qualities
Of anything that there is.

We may make an attribution,
Saying: "This is karma,"
But if we fall under the power of karma
We will not have self-originating wisdom.

Causes, in fact, resemble vajra problems.
This is unborn,
So it will not be destroyed.

Our hearts have been enlightened
Since the primordial.
Our dominion is not shaken
By thoughts of a search.
The mandala of wisdom

Is, in fact, a mandala.
It is through our thoughts
That the mandalas,
However many there may be,
Appear.

Mandalas come from mandalas.
All the mandalas of the Buddhas
Abide in the heart
That holds a mandala.

It is difficult,
Even for all the Buddhas,
To define this heart.
It is a mandala
That brings the three domains of obstruction
To their completion.

The enlightenment that comes to us
By means of excellent methods
Is, in fact, granted as a vajra empowerment.
It is truly a dominion of thusness.

Our thoughts,
As many as there are,
Are boundless.
The oral transmission
Of the vehicles of ideas
May be searched throughout
For some grand significance,
A heart-essence that is correct,
But we will not find it.

An equanimous mind
Has equanimity for all things.
It is the path to freedom.

Self-awareness is not stained
By any problems that may come
From exaggeration and denigration.
It is an unobstructed purity.

The holiest retreat practice
Is the mind.
This is the unmistaken pathway
Of those who have gone to bliss.
It is truly the dominion of thusness.

The Buddha speaks
Without exaggeration or depreciation.
This is the heart-essence
Of the meaning of the supreme secret.
It is the mandala of a heart of bliss.

Our own minds are stable,
And are wish fulfilling jewels
And wish fulfilling trees.
They have been empowered
For all our fields of practice.

This is a heart of excellence.
It is not a practice field for the critical.
The definition of the sky
Is that it is a totality
That is profound, vast, and spacious.
Wisdom unites with its own dominion.
This is how a dominion is effectively united with a dominion.

Our mind of itself has no base or root.
It is not masculine, feminine, or neuter.
It is not a dominion of color.
It is an abode for excellent virtues.
There is nothing that it does not move.
This is why people everywhere in the ten directions,
None excluded,
Are not killed or seized
By any Buddha.

This unborn and unending mandala
Is the essence or the fruition
Of both the things that transcend this world
And the things of this world.
This is why the mandala that has no cause or result
Is, in fact, a dominion that is not born
And does not end.

The embodiment of the unchanging swastika[35]
Stands within it.
It plays in the two great accumulations,[36]
And in their completion.

The visible mandala of wisdom
Is neither visible nor invisible.
It is also not divided
Between being existent and non-existent.

Self-awareness is primordially pure.
This heart-essence is without source.
It is unborn.
It is evident on account of its uncontrived and uncreated character.

Happiness and sorrow have a common cause.
Our soul[37] grants empowerment to our soul.
There is nothing that is destroyed,
And there is no destroyer.

A vajra soul[38] does not engage
In anything at all.

The Buddha has brought together
All the Dharmas,
With none excepted,
Into the heart-essence of enlightenment.

We look at everything,
Whether it is external or internal,
As an embodiment of the heart-essence of enlightenment.

Those who dwell on this path of excellence
Are forever freed from horrible lives,
And are on the level of enlightenment.

---

[35] gYung drung
[36] Merit and wisdom.
[37] bDag, Skt. Atman
[38] rDo rje'i bDag

There is no true nature to this.
It may appear to be anything.
One who remains in the unspeakable state
Where we let go of written words and grammar
Will not be stuck on grammar or words.
His heart will not dwell on a heart,
And there is nothing that will obstruct it.

From the Tantra of Great Bliss, this is chapter seventeen: The Heart-Essence of the Secret Upadeśa is Not Stained by Any Fault.

THE VIEW AND SAMAYA
OF THE SECRET UPADEŚA

Then the Blessed One, the All Good One, entered the equanimity of the samadhi of an endless view, and intentionally spoke on this topic:

Any names or conventionalities we may hold onto
In the world,
The identity of which
Is a mandala of illusion,
Are definitions
That are to be individually deconstructed.

Self-originating wisdom is most fortunate.
It does not exist.
It is not non-existent.
It is not to be visualized.
It has no true nature.
It is purity itself.
It was not created by anyone.
It is self-originating.

All things are of one taste in this dominion.
For a rich woman,
Whose dominion is just what it is,
Everything,
With no partitions,
Is the path to enlightenment.

Everything is born from out of the dominion of equality.
In just being born,
There is no birth.
Karma and the habitual tendencies of karma
Do not exist.
Our merit is the purity of all things.
We are not stained by anything.
We overcome everything.

The unchanging swastika
Is the embodiment of the great perfection.
This is also the level
On which there is no birth or death.
The dominion of the Dharma
And sentient beings
Are not two things.
In reality,
They are one.

The pair: Total purity and emotional problems
Are not to be separated.
They have a single character.
Their status has been determined:
They are unborn.
Emotional problems are not to be contrived to be remedies.
This is not a Dharma for the Materialists.[39]
This is a dwelling on what is,
Just as it is.

To have no I,
And no self,
Is to be the best of the Victorious Ones,
Those who are thoroughly cleansed
Of the causes and results that make up relative reality.
Emotional problems are, in fact, enlightenment.
Everyone,
With no exception,
Lives in bliss.

Then again the Blessed One, the All Good One, entered the equanimity
of the samadhi of essential purity, and he intentionally spoke on this topic:

---

[39] gDos po can

When we separate our dominion from our wisdom,
And our mind seeks origins and applications for its wisdom,
We work on meditation with the three kinds of samadhi.
We stop up the doors
To the five pathways of our emotional problems,
But when we are aware of our self-awareness itself,
The appearance of these five pathways
Is just an idea.

Both ideas and non-ideas are absent here.
The absence of both is, in fact, the correct path.
All the vehicles,
As bountiful as they are,
And none excepted,
Fail to speak according to the way that it is,
While our ideas,
As bountiful as they are,
Are the stages of our lungs,[40]
Which, in the same way, accommodate each one,
And illuminate them all.

The unsurpassed and supreme Vajrayana
Is, itself, the root of all things.
It is like water falling into
The space of the ocean.
The real essence of an ocean's water
Is that it is not to be condensed,
For it is condensed naturally.
Its real essence is a supreme vehicle.
The ocean is a lotus jewel.

Vajrasattva's true body
Does not move away from
The way things are.
It is like the light from the rising sun.
It shines on limitless living beings throughout the three worlds.

The fields of the Sugatas
Are an inconceivable enumeration of the vehicles
In which we do virtue.

---

[40] gLo, possibly to be read bLo, meaning mind or attitude.

It has never been proclaimed
That the things we do in the field of compassion
Are not meaningful.

Every teaching that accords with what is true
Brings together an understanding of this self-originating dominion.
Those who have stainless and pure intelligence
Are yogins who are fortunate.

We have nothing to generate with our samadhi.
We have nothing to study with our three wisdoms.
We have nothing to meditate on that uses the analytics of a view.
We have no mandala,
And have no mandala to meditate on.
All our fields of practice
Are primordially pure.

Self-originating wisdom
Wanders through the mandala in which all things are equal,
And all are without duality.
This is not to be contrived as being a path.

Then Vajradhara asked:

How are the samaya for the view to be divided,
And what is the best view?
Also, what is the best samaya?

Then the Blessed One, the All Good One, entered the equanimity of the samadhi that divides up the views and the samaya, and he intentionally spoke on this topic:

Ignorance, desire, hatred,
Pride, and jealousy:
These are the big five.
After we abandon them,
There will not be any nirvana.
Not abandoning them is, in fact, the path of enlightenment.

We will always use the five kinds of ambrosia.
Their virtues, just as they are,
Make them the finest of implements.
They are causes for our unsurpassed success.

We must eat them without regard to cleanliness or filth,
And we will acquire the jewel of Buddhahood.

Our own view is our samaya.
A view is not something that exists separately.
Samaya themselves have been proclaimed to be views.
This is why both views and samaya
Are to be retained on the unmistaken path.

Samaya is the supreme union,
While liberation is said to be the best view.
In union there is, in fact, liberation.
In liberation there is, in fact, union.
Union, liberation, views, and samaya:
These are the bases for emptying out
The places where life is horrible.

In an unsurpassed field
We brilliantly unite.
For those who are hot,
The medicine is to be cool.
For those that are cold,
There is the medicine of warmth.

Coolness and warmth,
Gentle and rough:
These have equal parts,
And this is how we demonstrate
The views that we understand.

In the brilliantly diffused pure lands of the Buddhas,
The mandalas of the Tathagatas do appear,
Along with their infinite manifestations.
But they appear due to the blessings there are
In the views.

The ten directions,
The four times,
And everything else
Appear to us individually,
As we define our own ideas.

It may also be that
Samaya are subsumed within our views.
When we understand the significance of our views
And of our samaya,
Our embodiment and our wisdom will be inconceivable.

When we understand the significance of self-aware wisdom,
We attain that swastika that has no birth or death.

Desire, hatred, and even ignorance
Emerge from the path of great enlightenment.
The five kinds of wonder there are in doing everything
Have also been proclaimed to be:
"Ornaments for reality's dominion."

The mudras of wisdom and magnificent methods
Also come from great enlightenment.
This has no border,
No center,
And no plurality.
It is totally pervasive,
While it does not go anywhere at all.
Yet in the same way,
It does not abide in anything.

We do not give birth to ideas about the sky,
While these speculations are indeed like the sky.
The unattached sky is free from blueness.
The sky appears to us
Due to our own personal interest.

From the Tantra of Great Bliss, this is chapter eighteen: The View and Samaya of the Secret Upadeśa.

THE GREAT MANDALA
OF THE SECRET UPADEŚA

Then Vajradhara asked:

Blessed One,
Please explain the significance of the two kinds of stainless mandalas.

Then the Blessed One, the All Good One, entered the equanimity of the samadhi that is elicited by the two kinds of mandalas, and the Tathagata's vajra body, speech, and mind brought out these forty-two letters. This is what emerged:

A Ka Kha Ga Gha Nga |
Tsa Tsha Dza Dzha Nya |
Ṭa Ṭha Ḍa Ḍha Ṇa |
Pa Pha Ba Bha Ma |
Ya Wa Ra La |
Śa Ṣa Sa Ha Kṣa |
I Ī | U Ū | E Ai | O Ou |
Dza: Hūṃ Baṃ Ho: |

The entire domain of this world
Rose up
To be a cause for this physical mandala.

The ten directions were shaken through the four times.
The three thousands,
The one thousand,

95

The two thousand,
And the five elements
Shook.
They shook to the extreme.
They totally shook.

Then the Blessed One spoke out intentionally on this topic:

The great mandala abides in our selves.
Our five heaps
Are the five perfect Buddhas.
All of our consciousnesses, generative forces, and domains
Are male and female Bodhisattvas.

The mothers of wisdom,
Whose domain is the sky,
Are the true essence of the uncorrupted mandala:
Earth and water are Eyes and Māmaki.
Fire and wind are White Garment and Tara.
They are primordially removed from the thousands of domains
That are in the ten directions.

The great mandala of self-originating life
Is that of the wrathful father and mother.
It has four gates.
The blazing light of this great mandala
Is the vast abode of Akaniṣṭa,
Which never stops moving through the ten directions,
And which has no border or center.

Our foundation is the brilliantly clear light
From the wheel of measureless wisdom.
It is immeasurable.
It transforms into a square.
There are four doors.
The designs around the doors
Are especially beautiful.
Their four magnificent facades
Are especially beautiful.

There are dismounting points, ladders,
Nets made of precious jewels,
Half-curtains, pearls, *Asma* dancers,

Bouquet carriers, and young lads.

There is a variety of music,
A variety of scent,
A variety of tastes,
And a variety of things to touch.
They appear in alignment with the ten directions.

The dominion of the immense palace
That appears there by itself
Is the dominion of the Victorious One's Dharma.
Its jewelry
Makes the blazing mandala of just what is
To shine.

In the immense palace of blazing wisdom,
A magnificent mandala with four corners,
There is a wheel with four spokes.
It has a band around the circumference.
The four corners are wondrous in their ornamentation.

The square is a totality.
The design around the doors is beautiful.
Using massive clouds of jewels and of music,
The mandala of blazing wisdom
Is ornamented,
As if it were a magnificent palace.

On top of thrones made of
Lions, elephants, horses, buffalo, and eagles,
There form seats,
Thrones that are ornamented by a sun, a moon, a lotus,
And a precious jewel.

The vajra king and queen
Have one face and two hands.
These four:
Earth Heart, Sky Heart, Avalokiteśvara, and Vajrapani,
Circle off to the right.
The four Bodhisattva mothers:
Lāsye, Māle, and the rest
Turn in a circle to the left.

On the corners there are these four:
Maitreya, the All Good One, the Remover of Obstacles, and Mañjuśrī.
The four goddesses of offering
Are arranged as in the above,
Starting from the right of Earth Heart.
Dispersed between them
We place the six Sages.

Then we place the male and female All Good Ones
Behind and in front of the vajra wheel.

Detailed to the doors,
There are the four wrathful ones.
On the right are the women.
On the left are the men.
Between the male and female wrathful ones
We place the four door-matrons in the middle.
The good women are in front.
The good men are behind.
The primary figure is white.
He is Vajradhara.

A yellow mirror spins in a circle.
There is a blazing jewel of verdant wisdom.
The wisdom of ideas is a red lotus.
The wisdom of success is a green crossed-vajra.
The precious pens are white and yellow.
The sword is dark blue.
The lotus is white.
The vajra is green.
The *naga* tree is red.
The wheel is orange.
The sheaves of grain are white.

Mañjuśrī is yellow.
He holds an utpala flower,
A white mirror and a blue rosary.
His tongue is red.
His fingers are whitish green.

The incense fire is yellow.
The flower is dark blue.
The lamps are bright red.

The perfumed water is green.
The burning one wears armor of yellow.
He holds a red book and a lake of jewels.
He anoints the Victorious Ones.

The fire-water is black.
The vajra is light yellow.
The club is dark blue.
The scorpion mudra is red.
The staff is green.

The wrathful women blaze in rage.
Their iron hooks are white.
Their nooses are yellow.
Their chains are red.
Their bells are green.
Their blazing mandala is unsurpassed.

This great mass of blazing light rays
Surrounds the great mandala in a circle.

Then the Blessed One, the All Good One, entered the equanimity of the samadhi of uttering the heart-spell of his speech, and this heart-spell of his speech emerged from his body, speech, and mind:

Brum Tsakra Biśuddhe | Hūm Vajrasatva Hūm | Om Bairotsana Dziga Om | Sva Ratna Sva | Am Amrita Am | Ha Praloki Ha | Mum Dhātu Śvari Mum | Lam Di Śvarati Lam | Mam Moharati Mam | Pyam Ragalogati Pyam | Tram Saha Hri Tram | Kṣa Garbha Kṣa | Tram A Garbhaya Tram | Hrī: Padma Padmo Hrī | Dzi Vajrapāṇi Dzi | Hūm Lāsye Samaya Ho | Tram Māle Samayastvam | Hrī: Girti Rago Ham | Anirtiya Svāhā | Mili Mahāyami Svāhā | Thlim Padra Thlim Svāhā | Hūm Kṣukhanggeya Svāhā |Mum Mañjuśrī Gaya Svāhā | Hedukrum Svāhā | Sapuṣpa Svāhā | Am Mayuke Sukeni A Svāhā | Ho Gandhe Tsitta Tratha Svāhā | Hūm Trailokya | Byīkatra Phaṭ | Hūm Yamānata Krida Phaṭ | Hūm Padmanata Krida Phaṭ | Bigananta Krida Phaṭ | Hūm Haprajñāta Krida Phaṭ | Om Dāramahā Ekrodhiśvari Dzvalani Phaṭ | Om Dāhimahāratna Ekrodhiśvari Dzvalani Phaṭ | Om Padmamahā Ekrodhiśvari Dzvalani Phaṭ | Om Karmamahā Ekrodhiśvari Dzvalani Phaṭ | Om Abamunekram Svāhā | Om Nṛi Munekrum Svāhā | Om Kṣam Sumune Bram Svāhā | Om Trimune Brum Svāhā | Om Pramune Kṣam Svāhā | Om Dudzamune Saśoka Svāhā | Om A A Samanta Heta Svāhā |

Vajrasatva Samanta Oṃ Hūṃ Hūṃ Vajra Vajra Dza Dza Kruda Svāhā |
Hūṃ Ñukarmaña Svāhā | Paṃ Padmakule Svāhā | Haṃ He Ha Ha Svāhā
|

This mandala of speech
Emerged from his body, speech, and mind,
So it is famed as his mandala
Throughout all the dominions of the world.

All of these magnificent mandalas
Were made to hold the mandalas of wisdom,
So the heart-spells of the five wisdoms
Were also made to melt into this:

Oṃ Tathāgato Jñāna Mahā Svabhāwa Atmako 'Haṃ
Oṃ Vajra Mahā Jñāna Svabhāwa Atmako 'Haṃ
Oṃ Ratna Mahā Jñāna Siddhi Vajra Svabhāwa Atmako 'Haṃ
Oṃ Padma Mahā Jñāna Anurakto Vajra Svabhāwa Atmako 'Haṃ
Oṃ Mahā Śunyatā Jñāna Karma Vajra Svabhāwa Atmako 'Haṃ

The heart-spells of the five wisdoms
Also emerged from his body, speech, and mind.
When they are recited
Light will shine,
And then will brilliantly dissolve.
The sounds of the heart-spells
Make all and everything luminous.

Within this magnificently blazing mandala,
The mandala comes from a mandala.
The mandala of a mandala has a mandala.
The true identity of the mandala of speech
Is perfected in its being a mandala
That blazes in so many ways.
Its luminescence is, in fact,
An embodiment of a vajra of speech.

We imagine that the heart-spell
Of the lineage of two tens,
And the five particulars,
Is just the size of a sesame seed,
And the sun and the moon
Are just the size of turnip seeds.

We position ourselves above them,
And work on uniting.

We work on reciting the heart-spell
As we circle in a dance.
On the right meridian we place Hūṃ.
On the left meridian we place Muṃ.
The two unite.
They subsume each other,
And in the way of clapping,
We are entwined into non-duality.

The mandala is effulgent.
Our right forefinger is a blazing Oṃ.
Our left points in a Lam.
We control the Hūṃ, Muṃ, and the rest.

Then, in the way of clapping,
We are non-dual.
We are entwined,
And this makes the mandala glow.

The ten fathers and mothers blaze.
Entwined in pairs,
They glow.

We imagine that the first letter Oṃ,
And the rest of the four,
Are just the size of mustard seeds.

We place there the four classes of written letters,
Beginning with the gutturals,[41]
Just the size of sesame seeds.

On the knuckle of the first finger of our hand,
We make an arrangement as in the above,
Using arrogance and the other four attitudes.
We do this in the way of clapping.

When we clap,
The two are brought together,

---

[41] mThong byed. These are usually Ka Kha Ga Gha and Nga.

To overcome each other.
We are entwined in non-duality,
So our mandala glows.

We imagine that there is a sun
At the root of the Oṃ,
A blazing letter Oṃ,
Just the size of a small pea.
We imagine that the heart-spell of wood
Is on top of this,
Just the size of a white mustard seed.

In the space below the Hūṃ
We imagine the heart-spell for sheaves of grain,
Just the size of a mustard seed.

In the space below the Oṃ,
We imagine the heart-spell of a wheel,
Just the size of a mustard seed.

In the space below the Ha
We also imagine the heart-spell of an utpala flower.

In the space of the Lam,
We place the moon.

Then we must imagine
The heart-spell of incense.

In the space below the Muṃ
We must imagine the heart-spell of flowers.

In the space below the Pyaṃ
We must imagine the heart-spell for oil lamps.

In the space below the Traṃ
We must imagine the heart-spell of scent.

The eight male Bodhisattvas,
And eight female Bodhisattvas,
Join their palms,
And entwine in father-mother union,
Until they control all others.

Delusions of a duality
Are a blazing light.
It makes this magnificent mandala glow.

The tip of the Sva is blazing,
And its edges are greater than
The pinnacle of the sun.
In its middle are the humans.
The asuras are on the side.
On the summit of the moon
There are the animals.
The hungry ghosts are between.
The hells are placed lower.
They are placed there in the style of a drama,
Fitting for the audience.

At the root of the Oṃ of the sun
There is Vijaya.[42]
At the root of the Lam of the moon
There is the lady Vijaya.

At the summit of the Hūṃ of the sun
There is an iron hook.
At the root of the Muṃ of the moon
There is a noose.

At the root of the Aṃ of the sun
There is an executioner.
At the root of the Byaṃ of the moon
There is a lady executioner.

At the root of the Ha of the sun
There is Hayagriva.
At the root of the Ha of the moon
There is the lady Hayagriva.

In the depths of the sun
There are iron chains.
In the depths of the moon
There is a blazing bell.

---

[42] rNam rgyal

Between the root and the depth
Of the Sva of the sun,
An entwining light blazes forth,
And becomes special.

In the depths of the moon
There is the lady of entwinement.[43]
When the father and the mother
Join with each other,
Each controlling the other,
The mandala of their union
Is a blazing light.

We imagine that the entire mandala is glowing.

We meditate on a body,
The heart-essence of which is Hūṃ.
We suck our two hands,
And on top of them we draw the mandalas
For four individual beings.

We place a vase that is filled
With the five essences
In the center of the mandala.

For the great mandalas and their kind,
We use brilliant ornamentation,
With ornaments above,
Ornaments below,
And ornaments in-between,
To present a style of ornamentation.

We surround it with
An assortment of food and drink of many flavors,
An assortment of garments, boots, and hanging adornments,
And an assortment of the specific items used for offerings,
Then we offer it with our samadhi.

Offering without being conscious of it
It said to be the greatest offering,

---

[43] 'Khyil ma

So when we make offerings and such things,
We use great offerings.

There are measurements for producing
A mandala of a physical image,
But those who are so endowed
Will use the presence of samadhi.

The rituals for the levels,
And such things,
And the stages for painting on
The insignia of a drop,[44]
According to the way of great things,
Such as mandalas,
Is that the mandala of merit
Is summoned from the mandala
Used for the correct granting of an empowerment.

The first great mandala
Is our engagement in our guru's mind,
And then the students enter,
And we grant the empowerment.

The extent of our ability
Will be whatever we prefer.
We apply our experience.

So it is that for a great mandala
A great empowerment must be imparted.
The skillful will use any mandalas we wish:
One mandala, or three, or five,
Nine, or thirteen, and so on.

We imagine an embodiment of our lineage
At the center,
And then arrange the male and female Bodhisattvas.
Another way is to arrange things in a way we find mentally agreeable.
Another way is to arrange a consorted couple.
Another way is that of a great mandala,
With a center and spokes,
Which may fit with any meditation we may be doing.

---

[44] Thig

105

It is proclaimed that we must use wrathful ones
To act as door protectors.
It is proclaimed that the great mandala of the wrathful ones
Is also to be done in this way.

A totality of varied things will appear,
But there is no mandala
That appears by its own nature.
This, indeed, has been described to be wisdom.

From the Tantra of Great Bliss, this is chapter nineteen: The Great
Mandala of the Secret Upadeśa.

THE SPONTANEOUS PRESENCE
OF THE PERFECTION OF ALL THE UPADEŚA,
COMPLETE WITH NOTHING LEFT OUT

Then the Blessed One entered the equanimity of the samadhi that is spontaneously realized, and intentionally spoke on this topic:

All of the horrible existences,
None excepted,
Are our domains,
And while our senses are pure,
They are polluted by our conditions,
And we become unstable.

We understand forms and such things
To be selves.
This is the gradual development of the abodes of Brahma.[45]

When we do not understand equanimity or form
We do not understand that there is no supporting basis for names.
Our abode is transformed,
And from out of the four generative forces,[46]
We are born into a place
At the summit of the world.

---

[45] The abodes of Brahma is generally a reference to friendliness, compassion, joy, and equanimity.
[46] sKye mched

So it is that birth and all the rest
Are inconceivable.
No one whosoever created them.
They exist naturally.
There is nothing whatsoever that contrives
The mandala of natural luminescence.
It is not polluted.

If we understand that there is no duality,
Then who will do the contriving?
Who will understand?

This is not something that is shared in common
With anyone.

Of all the Dharmas that appear to resemble this,
And all the Buddhas of the ten directions
And the four times,
There is not even one
That is apart from his soul.[47]

They are held by the highness and lowness of their vehicles.
Their bodies are maintained
As if they were Buddhas,
Or male and female Bodhisattvas incarnate.

This is a space of equanimity
In which subjects and objects are not a duality.
Everything turns out to be a state of equanimity.
All the mandalas, external and internal,
And the sounds and entities,
However many there may be,
Are all perfected
Within the heart-essence of our gathering.

An analogy is that
Just as a dancer
Shows collections of undamaged shapes
From out of her hands,
Our undamaged bodies
Are made fully luminescent

---

[47] bDag, Atman.

By a heart of effortless and supreme perfection.

When we do not attribute this to be any self or other,
We fully retain the mandala in its entirety.

All things are in the dominion
Of their own occurrence.
In their variety,
They shine out like lightening.
In this very shining,
They are like rainbows.

There is no true nature to this.
It is All Good.
This, in fact, has been described to be
The embodiment of the Dharma.
Embodied in its totality,
Our lineage is bountiful.

The eight secret charnel grounds are quiet.
The sounds of entities
Come from non-entities.
Assortments of yoga
Are quiet and empty.
Assortments of Dharma
Are perfected in our minds.

The heaps of Dharmas
Are perfected in this domain.
Just as the sun, the moon,
And all the planets and stars
Are perfected in the unvisualized bounty of the sky,
And then the dominion of the sky
Is perfected in purity.
The heaps and the domains are, in fact, Dharmas.

The mandala of the Dharma
Is perfected in the Dharma.
There is nothing to exemplify
By saying: "This."

The act of exemplification
Is a conceptual construct.

Until we have finished with conceptual constructs,
However many there may be,
We will not find the path of the Buddha's enlightenment.

The embodiment of the Dharma
Is not an idea.
It is not an equanimity.
We do not hold onto it
By grasping at it.
It is like a water-moon.

By the playfulness of the All Good One,
The vowels and consonants have been profoundly explicated.
Origins and applications,
As we understand them,
Are like the little monkeys that hit the ground
After the humans have left.
There is a lot of work to be done,
While there is no self.
It is by the power of our self-awareness
That we receive empowerment.

The yoga of definitions
Is just an idea.
It dwells in the space of a great equanimity.
Consciousness and considerations,
In all their variety,
Are presented to be an unmoving and self-originating circle.

There is no I or self in this.
It is not dirtied by the dust of conditions.
It is naturally pure,
So everything is, in fact,
The heart-essence of the one who moves in bliss.

Where would we go?
What would we be born as?
There is no substance which is born into the world.
The great garudas soar through the sky.
And the nagas who live in the ocean are destroyed,
For the body of the garuda of itself is not acceptable to them.

The supreme Vajrayana is unsurpassed.
It is effortless.
It does not fail.
It brings everything together.
It destroys ideas.
It decimates the levels.
All the vehicles,
None excepted,
Are devoured in its stomach.

This dominion is beyond our thoughts,
But there are innumerable statements about it
That say: "This."
This is why there are no Tantras in written letters.

There is no meditation.
The sky is beyond deeds,
So we do not seek.
We do not practice.
We do not shift.

We must finish up with our ways of meditation.
We must overcome our ways of practice.
The heart-essence of self-awareness does not move,
So who would want it for a path of discovery?

Those who maintain the purity in their dominion of equanimity
Are the same as the ones that mount oxen,
Then work with what follows.
After they are thrown off,
They seek for Buddhahood.

E Ma'o!
This is the practice field of the Buddhas!
It is not a place that we will find
By searching for it.
There are no objects
That accord with the six Dharmas.
We are like blind people,
Scrutinizing the sky.

The path of purity that goes higher and higher
Is in agreement with the effortless Dharma,

But if we travel toward it on a path,
We will not see it,
As if it were the end of the sky.

In the heart-essence of perfected primordial equanimity,
There is nothing that must be practiced or protected.
There is neither liberation nor non-liberation.
This is beyond our ideas of virtue and non-virtue.

Causes and results are inseparable.
There is no freedom or enlightenment to be achieved
Through working on rejecting the five kinds of emotional problems.

This is the river of primordial thusness.
We will not find the path of the perfect Buddha
Through austerities, travelling, protecting, trying, or seeking.
Using vows, our root enlightenment is distant.
Using roots of virtue,
We build a basis for the birth of sorrow.
This also makes us be born into a horrible life.

When we enact union with prostitutes,
Or take the lives of all sentient beings,
We practice disgusting things
On the very level of the All Good One,
And we are extremely happy.

From the Tantra of Great Bliss, this is chapter twenty: The Spontaneous Presence of the Perfection of All the Upadeśa, Complete with Nothing Left Out.

THE SECRET UPADEŚA HAVE NO VIEWPOINT

Then the Blessed One, the All Good One, entered the equanimity of the samadhi that does not look into the variety of views, and intentionally spoke on this topic.

There is no outside or inside.
This is the space of great wisdom.
Everything is truly within everything.
This is the embodiment of glory.
It is the natural mandala
That is perfection itself.

It follows that with spontaneously realized perfect equanimity
Objects and awareness are not two things.
There is no earlier or later.
This is the dominion of the way it is.

There is no result
In which someone like Vajrasattva
Is visible to our sight.

Gathering and not gathering,
Dwelling and not dwelling:
These are not the root.
They are causes for downfalls.
We even count levels,
And bow to applications.

Generation, practice, and worship
Are inherently pure,
So they are inherently present.

We do not need austerities or difficult practices.
We do not need to use levels and quests to seek things.
This is unsurpassed wisdom.

We do not need to count it,
Or to honor its applications.
This is effortless.
It is beyond our deeds.

We do not need to generate,
To practice,
Or to do anything.
This is the unborn space of bliss.

When we worship,
There is no Victorious One to worship.
This is a supreme victory,
An embodiment of perfection.
It is not necessary to exemplify it in writing.

This is the naturally clear light.
We do not need to praise or blame it.

This is beyond the shapes of our heaps.
It is beyond the lights of the five wisdoms.

This is not a color or a shape.
When we look at this,
There is nothing to see.

It is, itself, beyond the word "view."
In this there are no causes or results.
Its excellence is that nothing whatever divides it.
This is called "a gathering."
It brings everything together,
Like the wind from the ocean.

There is not anything that really exists,
So a variety of non-entities

Is what actually appears.
In this appearance
There is nothing at all.

We may practice all variety of vehicles,
But their lack of reality is, itself, correct.
The best of results
Is not to be bothered by heroes.[48]
This is the way of Vajrasattva himself.

Our happiness in the present,
And that which is later,
Are either directly perceived,
Or come from behind.
There are problems with this,
So we must not rely on it.

This has been our heart-essence from the primordial,
So the three times are one.
There is no difference.

For Bodhisattvas,
Lords,
And All the Victorious Ones in their fields,
With none excepted,
The great perfection is the great perfection.
It is beyond thought,
Unspeakable,
The supreme path.
It is the basis of the ten perfections.

According to the conventions of the supreme siddhas,
Exaggeration, depreciation, and the four yogas
Are completely pure embodiments
That are primordially stamped with the seal.

It is open.
It is open.
The three realms are primordially awake and open.

---

[48] dPa' bo, Skt. Vīra

It is spoken.
It is spoken.
This mighty lord of virtues
Is beyond the conventions of speech.
It is unspeakable.

Even in our meditation,
We have ideas about ideas.
The embodiment of self-awareness
Is actually not to be meditated upon,
And not to be sought.

We settle into our natural condition,[49]
The thusness of the way it is.
This settling is also a settling
That is not a settling.
The thing that we settle into
Is the heart of Vajrasattva.
The Buddha himself does not have
A teaching that says: "This."

From the Tantra of Great Bliss, this is chapter twenty-one: The Secret Upadeśa Have no Viewpoint.

---

[49] Gyi nar

THE WAY IT IS WITH THE SECRET UPADEŚA

The Lord of Secrets, Vajradhara, asked:

Blessed One,
What is thusness?
Please explain this.

The Blessed One, the Lord of Bliss, the All Good One, entered the equanimity of the samadhi on the varieties in just what is, and intentionally spoke on this topic.

E Ma'o!
The true essence of the totality of the many things
Is unborn,
From the primordial.
It is the Bodhicitta,
Pure in every way.
Its true nature is indivisible.

The primordial and the ending are not to be divided.
From the beginning,
They are the same.
This is the ocean of the Victorious Ones.

The three times and the three existences
Are of essence an equality.
From the beginning,
The wisdom of the All Good
Has been the supreme dominion.

It has no clear divisions,
So there is no good or bad,
Nothing to take up or to reject.
We do not come or go,
So the three times are perfected
Instantaneously.

This mandala emerges from total equanimity.
The true nature of wisdom
Is in our own ideas.
We have nothing to say about
A wisdom that is not born from ideas.

The heart that does not divide between self and other
Has true wisdom.
When we do not see this heart-essence,
And have not studied any higher knowledge,
We search for something else.

We may teach sentient beings
Who are in the dark,
But they will not hear.
We may exemplify,
But they will not see.
They seek their true selves
In something else,
So they do not become Buddhas.

We do not see any teachers
That are not like this.
They desire to have a path,
So they travel along a path.
They desire to travel,
But they are unable to go.

The true meaning is hidden,
So nobody sees it.
What is this knowledge?
What are these practices?
Who can know?

We work to sit naturally.[50]

This is superior to work and deeds.
The practices in someone's mind
Become the practices of enlightenment.

If we do not give up the definitions
That are the ideas and practices of our intellects,
We will not remember,
And we will not discern,
That the cause of our spinning
Is that we did not give them up.

The uncorrupted, undivided, directly perceived Buddha
Does not exemplify
That there is any significance to our cravings for this.
Anyone who practices to this extent,
Using the awareness of the intellect,
Is practicing a real form
For the clouds in the sky.

How can we understand that there is no sky?
A cloud appears,
But it is not possible that it be covered.

In *swastika* Buddhahood,
Which is completely pure,
Everything is equal,
From the beginning,
And is completely pure.

When we abide on the plain level of non-conceptualization,
This state makes us understand
That the selfless great spirit[51]
Is the origin of all things.
That is why the uncontrived path of the Victorious Ones
Is an unsurpassed wisdom that is unstoppable,
And has no cause or origin.

It does not examine,
And there is no practice.
This is beyond the powers

---

[50] Gyi nar
[51] bDag med bdag chen

Of the methods that hold to a self.
It is an abode of knowledge,
Just as it is.

There does not exist a proclamation by anyone
That teaches about this kind of great spirit.
The way that it is
Is the correct path to enlightenment.
The best life is to have nothing to take up,
And nothing to cast off.
It is unsurpassed.

This is the *dhāraṇī* for the unmoving.
We do not join or part from it.
The wisdom that understands
Is a treasure of wish-fulfilling jewels.
It is difficult to teach,
And it is not appropriate to change its meaning.

Who is it that appears
As if he were an image in a mirror?
Holiness is not taught to be something like this.
There is no extremely clear awareness
That resembles ignorance.
It is difficult to teach the specifics
On the holy retention of jewels,
For they are like seals stamped
On the opening of an iron box.

Our true heart-essence is luminous,
Without external or internal shadows.
This is a totally unmistaken view,
Just as it is.

Do not abandon samsara!
Suffering is the path of enlightenment.
This is beyond our fields of practice:
Views and what we must view.

The holder of the lamp of wisdom
Is beyond delusion.
Great compassion churns the wisdom of playfulness.
This is beyond meditation, practice, thought, and speech.

A Buddha is a Buddha,
Just as he is.

A mind of thusness,
Where just what is
Is just like that,
Is a stable and unchanging magnificent samaya.
The lamp of a spacious heart has been blazing,
From the beginning.
This is amazing and astounding.
It is a magnificent playfulness.
The world has been an effortless sky-space,
From the beginning.

Self-aware wisdom arises
From out of the state of ignorance,
Without our visualizing anything at all,
And when it does,
Thusness is a pathway that accommodates sentient beings.

The true nature of all living things is thusness.
Children who do not understand adulterate it,
On account of their delusions.
This is the same as when
The medicine itself seeks the doctor.

The wisdom of self-awareness
Is an unchanging river of bliss.
It is the way things are
When we do not abide
In either the external or the internal.

It is difficult to tach this
By saying: "This,"
And there is nothing in-between.

From the Tantra of Great Bliss, this is chapter twenty-two: The Way It Is with the Secret Upadeśa.

THE OCCASION FOR EMPOWERMENT INTO THE SECRET UPADEŚA

Then the Blessed One, the All Good One, entered the equanimity of the samadhi of imparting empowerment, and intentionally spoke on this topic.

The perfect empowerment of wisdom
Is the king of self-awareness himself.
The wheel that enacts the empowerment
Is an unattached foundation
For our abiding in equanimity.

The total clarity of self-awareness
Grants the empowerment of wisdom.
In the way that it is,
Self-awareness abides in thusness.

This thusness is inconceivable
In its expansion and contraction.
This is the body of bodies:
An embodiment that transmits a variety of empowerments.
The king of self-awareness
Grants empowerment to the three existences.[52]

The best empowerment
Is enacted by playfully bringing everything together.

---

[52] Srid gsum. This may refer to beings that live under the ground, on its surface, or in the air.

The perfect empowerment
Is the effortless path that resembles ignorance.

All the mandalas of the Buddhas,
None excepted,
Are embodiments of the Victorious Ones.
When we do not work to focus our consciousness
On the five bodies, the five wisdoms,
The empowerment, or on the Dharma,
That is the best of the best.
When we do not work to focus on the empowerment,
That is the best empowerment.
The mandala that subsumes the many things
Is the best mandala.
To dwell in the perfection of these three things that are the best
Is the best empowerment.

From the beginning,
We have not dwelt on any conventional name,
For the past, the future, and the present are not definite.
While we designate something to have no birth or ending,
There is a body that unites the three great times.

We are primordially equanimous,
So there is no gradual presentation.
This is not singular or plural.
It is beyond positions.

The empowerment in which we set out ornaments,
Things we have accumulated as offerings,
Is spontaneously perfected,
And is naturally present.
There is nothing that obstructs it.
Because it is spontaneously present,
We do not dedicate.
We do not think.
This is pure from the primordial,
So it is our ambrosia.

Even the special qualities of the twelve generative forces[53]
Are spontaneously realized by their very nature.

---

[53] 'Du mched bcu gnyis.

The wisdom of the three embodiments
Arises under the circumstance of the empowerment.
The empowerment is also perfect.

There are no five empowerments
That are to be received through some higher thinking.

From the Tantra of Great Bliss, this is chapter twenty-three: The Occasion for Empowerment into the Secret Upadeśa.

THE TOPIC OF THE SECRET UPADEŚA IS BEYOND THOUGHT AND IS UNSPEAKABLE

Then Vajradharma Vajradhara asked the Blessed One, the All Good One himself:

Please teach us the meaning of being unthinkable and unspeakable.

The Blessed One, the All Good One, entered the equanimity of the samadhi where there is no thought, and intentionally spoke on this topic:

I bow to the unspeakable state that is beyond thought!
I bow to the supreme teacher of teachers!
I bow to the unparalleled pathway,
That path that is praised by all!
I bow to the heart-essence of the Dharma,
Just as it is!
I bow to the river that holds effortless knowledge!
I bow to that body that holds primordial knowledge,
Just as it is!

All that makes up a supreme practice:
Total liberation through the levels,
The rule of the way,
And all the rest:
These are the mothers of the Sugatas.

The path of supreme liberation that accommodates everyone
Is actually Buddhahood.

This is subtle,
And difficult to understand.
It is a path for everyone.
Non-conceptualization is beyond our ideas.
Without this, that will not occur.
So it is with the path of supreme liberation.

This is not to be visualized.
It is not static.
It is uncomplicated.
It is beyond all our thoughts.
Words will not strike at it.
It is not a shape or color
That is in the domain of our senses.

This is firm.
It is difficult to teach.
There is not even an atom to be said of it.
It is not a path that is to be taught
By saying: "This."

It is not singular.
It is not plural.
After we have used logic to deconstruct it,
We continue to use what it means in what we do.

The things the meditators
Who were the Rishis of old
Believed to be real meditation
Were deviant in specific ways,
And they were ill.
The path of attachment to meditation is a disease,
And it finished them off.

The intent of their debased practices
Is not in the scriptures.
It is a delusion.
They believe that there is a path of practice
At the end of words,
But the causes and results that they think about
Resemble chasing after an optical illusion.

To use profound understandings
To seek for unsurpassed Buddhahood
Is extremely easy.

This does not come from anyone else.
It is just what it is.
We believe it to be superior.

The correct path to enlightenment
Is not to be exemplified in words.
If we look at what they truly are,
They are delusions.

The path of equality is neither pure nor impure.
Ignorance and wisdom are not to be divided
In any way at all.

To be without moving or shaking
By one's very character
Is to live as a king of samadhi.

There is no visualization that we look at
And say: "I see it this way."
It is the eye that sees things directly,
And this is why we call it:
"The eye of omniscience."

It has no border or center,
So it is called: "Naturally spacious."

Without acquiring anything,
Or rejecting anything,
We achieve the king of equanimities.

Our minds and our habitual tendencies
Are not two things.
They are mixed, and they are equal.
They appear to us when we grasp at them.

We do not throw out or reject
Any of the dharmas that are permanent.
We use the method
In which no form of any kind is necessary

For this self-originating reality,
And we play within it.

The Dharmas that are totally rejected,
And that no one accepts:
The five emotional problems
And the five inexpiables,
Are paths of purity.
When we enter them
We attain the king of equanimities.

Do not abandon anyone,
Be they women or anyone else!

We may put the meanings
Of the accounts of the years
Of our five emotional problems
And our five inexpiables
Into our logical intellects,
And we may define the three kinds of samadhi,
Making use of philosophical theories,
But we will be deviating from the transmission of effortlessness.
This is a delusion.

We dwell in the land
Of effortless and spontaneously perfected bliss.
This is the heart-essence of the greatness
Of our wisdom's self-origination.
It is not to be visualized.
It does not move.
It is beyond any report.

We abide totally within a transmission
That is already beyond our works,
Just as it is.
It is a state that is unborn and does not stop,
Like the sky.
It is not to be taught
By saying: "This."
It is the embodiment of the one circle.[54]
It does not expand or contract.

---

[54] Thig le

It is the path of freedom:
Holiness itself.

This is not an idea.
It is not a conceptualization.
It is beyond wisdom and methods.
It has no extremes.
It has no center.
There are no instructions on its essence.

It is uncontrived,
Like the sky.
It is beyond the objects that we talk and think about.
It is immeasurable.
Its magnificent significance has no exemplar.
It is the Victorious One's heart.
It is the river of perfect enlightenment.
It is difficult to teach it
By saying: "This."

The All Good
Is a great bliss that is sure.
We place ourselves thusly, like this,
And we do not seek for it,
For it is not to be sought.
This is why the mother of the Sugatas
Is a light that is totally victorious.

Fortunately,
This is not to be exemplified in writing.
It is beyond conventionalities,
For it is not possible
That Vajrasattva leave his body behind.
Whatever he does,
He is the character of the All Good One.
He is the Victorious One.
He does not meditate or practice.
His ideas are unsurpassed.

Do not cling to words!
Do not hold onto what your ears hear!
This is the path of enlightenment!

When we do not depend on anyone,
And have no views or direct perceptions,
That is the best practice.
The circle of the holy truth
Is beyond shapes and names,
So we have nothing to meditate on.

The Rishi meditators practice a path of desire,
And a path of deviant cravings.
To maintain quietude and seclusion,
Without an overabundance of words,
Clears away the sickness of delusion.

The most excellent king of medicine
Is expert in the special pathways.
He will remove the disease.
We will take our denseness and instability
As a path,
And we will heal.

You are the doctor Bodhisattva
Who makes us heal.
O Maker of Happiness,
I bow to you.

From the Tantra of Great Bliss, this is chapter twenty-four: The Topic of the Secret Upadeśa is Beyond Thought and is Unspeakable.

THE SECRET UPADEŚA
HAVE NO CONTEMPLATIONS OR MEDITATIONS

Then the Blessed One entered the equanimity of the samadhi in which there are no thoughts, and he intentionally spoke on this topic:

The unborn Bodhicitta
Is the basis for the many things.
It is not to be exemplified by saying: "This."
It is the embodiment of Buddhahood.

When we do not practice philosophical theoretics,
That is the best approach.
When we have no thought whatsoever,
That is contemplation.
The holy Bodhicitta,
The Buddha,
And our own minds
Appear to be different,
As does lightening,
But this is how we settle into our own natural state.[55]

We may meditate and contemplate,
But this is beyond the objects of our thought.
The self-awareness of the Sugata
Is self-arising,
And settles into its own peace.

---

[55] Gyin 'dar

Not to think anything at all
About the heart-essence of thusness,
And not to define anything:
This is how we must think.

There is no essence to our thoughts,
Whatsoever.
We do not seek them as our objects,
And we must not look for them anywhere else.
The heart-essence of self-awareness
Is to be sought in the space of self-awareness,
But if we seek for this self-awareness,
As something that is definitely present,
This presence will surely be beyond
Any words we may compose.
Our composition will also have no teaching
That says: "This."

To think or not to think:
This is how we must think.

Then the Blessed One entered the equanimity of the samadhi that
makes us excellent, and he intentionally spoke on this topic:

When the judgments of our minds
Do not appear,
This is itself
An unsurpassed heart.
This is a reality for which
There are no teachings.

It is a space that we do not work to transcend.
It is the path of the supreme and perfect heart.
It will not be grasped by wisdom and means.
It does not present a mudra.
It is beyond any embodiment.

From the beginning,
Our mudra is not visible.
There are no contemplations for it.
Not contemplating is, in fact,
The best contemplation.

The magnificent methods of the Bodhisattvas,
Who have finished all their quests,
And have transcended karma,
Are beyond our thoughts,
For they are victorious.

Coupled consorts
Are subject to interpretation,
And might not be holy.

He who has a blazing light in his heart
Will have the heart of the Dharma.
The noble path is not distant.
It is a path of splendor.
The noble ones all dwell on high.

This is not taught in the scriptures,
For there is nothing to teach.
The one who manifests in the center,
Among the perfect Buddhas
Is indeed a Buddha of patience.

E Ma'o!
There is not even an atom of conventionality in this,
So there is nothing to exaggerate or depreciate.
This is not some object
To be heard about or visualized.
There is nothing here that must be studied.

The Bodhicitta has no limits.
It is beyond the things we talk about,
However many there may be.

There is no basis on which to put a name.
Not being mistaken
Regarding the penetration of the doors
Is the best form of holiness.

It is not necessary to establish
That there are two kinds of truth.
There is not even an atom of this
To be exemplified in writing.

E Ma'o!
This field of practice for our minds
Is difficult to define.
It does not exist.
It does not exist even in the thoughts of the Rishis.

This unthinkable circle is beyond discussion.
It is inappropriate to think about it,
Saying: "This is enlightenment!"

We have dwelt in its equanimity
From the beginning.
It is the finest of hearts.
It is pristine,
But there is nothing to think about it.

In the same way that the wind and the water
Do not stir inside a well,
When we do not make up a view that says: "This,"
Regarding viewpoints,
And we do not move toward something else,
That will be our attainment of a heart of excellence.

This attainment is, itself,
Not something to be desired.
When we settle into a place
Where the five are blazing,
And are equanimous in the luminescence
Of the circle of wisdom,
We will achieve this heart-essence
In only a moment,
Rather than seeking for it
For a hundred hundred-thousand eons.

The ambrosial Bodhicitta
Has no thoughts.
It does not think.
It has no meditation.
It is beyond the words "wisdom" and "methods."

For these reasons
There is no Buddhahood in the mind.

It does not move from within.
It is not a place that we can seek.

From the Tantra of Great Bliss, this is chapter twenty-five: The Secret
Upadeśa Have No Contemplations or Meditations.

THE CONTENTS OF THE TANTRA

Then the Blessed One entered the equanimity of the samadhi that is free from every Dharma, and he intentionally spoke on this topic:

E Ma'o!
It is because we are travelling toward high status
That we do not find the path to enlightenment.
It is because we dwell in an unmoving nature,
That we do not use any great medicine.

It is because of the disease of the three poisons
That we never have the chance to be alive.
To hope that our delusional ideas will be a path
Is a river of shadows.

The desire that we become enlightened
On account of our searching for it
Is a topic for conceptualizations.
The best happiness
Is not a topic for our thoughts or our speech.

Delusions about enlightenment are always hungry.
They devour the Dharma.
Those who keep to the topics of these views
Do not see the Buddha.

The desire for enlightenment is a flawed understanding.
There is no Buddha.
The perfect Sugata is not to be visualized

As being anyone at all.

The Buddha is our teacher,
But to attribute a name to him is a mistake.
The use of words in relative reality
Is a river of ideas.

We may find Dharmas,
Be they Buddhist or Non-Buddhist,
But they will contradict the ones
That are said to have been proclaimed
From the mouth of our teacher.
These teachers and teachings
Do not find any path to enlightenment.

This thing that has no birth or ending,
That we do not visualize,
And is not present,
Is not something to talk or think about.
Neither is there anything proclaimed about it.

If the path of enlightenment was to be found
Just because our teacher proclaimed it,
There would be a transmission by stages
From the teacher of our teacher,
And it would be impossible for the Buddha
To attain Buddhahood,
Even in an eon.

Dispel the disease of searching!
This has been effortless from the beginning.
When we are infected with the disease of searching
Our deluded hearts become obstacles.

This is like the sky.
It has no true nature.
Groups will form that use words,
Such as "planet" and "star,"
But there is no end to them,
And they will not be depleted.
There is no final depletion of them.

We may profess anything,
And anything may happen,
But to attribute it to the Vinaya,
Or to the Sutra literature,
Is a mistake.

From its very depths,
This does not have anything
To be done on the stages of the vehicles.

The Buddha has no father,
No mother,
And no children.
He also has no Dharma.
He has no Three Jewels.
He has no practice field for his senses.
He has no form.

There is nothing that may be described to be
An embodiment of the Dharma.
This, however, is deep.

As if they were moons on a mirror of water,
Hosts of gods have appeared to explain this.
Their vehicles are inconceivable.
They have turned the things
That have been explained by an embodiment of the Dharma
Into a mere semblance,
Something that accords with them individually.
Their explanations come from someone else,
So the hopes that we attain them
Are Dharmas of delusion.

The hope to acquire Buddhahood
From someone else
Is an erroneous path.

It is not necessary
To practice these miserable austerities.
Prioritizing causes,
Such as the gathering of the accumulations,
Is a path of delusion.

This is spacious.
It is magnificent.
It is the great Dharma,
The Dharma of the heart.

It is a cure for the desire
To travel and study in smallness.
Greatness is not to be visualized.
If we think that it is an aspect of smallness,
We will be lost on the pathway
Where we travel through great and small.

From the beginning,
This has not been a Dharma
That refers to what was proclaimed,
Or was not proclaimed,
What is vast,
What is to be visualized,
Or what appears.
This is spontaneously perfected.

This is not to be connected with anyone
Who teaches by saying: "This."
There is nothing to be understood
Through it being taught.
There are no words to say.

This is not a dharma that is born or passes away.
It appears in its oneness.[56]
This oneness is also a bounteous root of roots.
It is the origin of our heart's true nature.
It is none other than the embodiment of the Dharma.

This spacious heart
Is not conceived through a direct experience
Of any kind.
There is no object to be apprehended.
There is also no abode of the mind.
The embodiment of the Dharma is all-encompassing,
So there is no Dharma that might be taught.

---

[56] gCig pu

We dwell as we are,
In a land that appears by itself,
And is not a visualization,
But with the disturbance from a single minute atom,
We lose all of the ten directions.
It is not appropriate to pile atoms into lumps.

The four times, in fact,
Also do not exist.
There is nowhere that we see anything amazing.
The eye that sees this
Has no form for its form,
So there is also nowhere for its essence.

This has no embodiment.
It may appear to be embodied,
But its body has no limbs.
Its limits are not to be exemplified.
This is why there are no writings in this dominion.

This Dharma is difficult to teach.
It is like listening to a corpse.
There is nothing to be said.

This is a place of natural greatness.
It is a place for all things,
Just as they are.

This is the emptiness of the empty.
Emptiness does not exist, either.
The dominion of the Dharma that is like the sky
Does not exist.
Wisdom is free.

There is no object to hold onto
As a meditation.
There is nothing to work out
In our minds.
There is nothing whatsoever to teach.
There is no heart of hearts.
Teaching this Dharma in a variety of ways
Is a deviant pathway.

There is nowhere that we can settle down
With the thought that our nature is the sky.
This is difficult to scrutinize,
Even with our most extremely quick thoughts.

The five emotional problems have been,
From the beginning,
The finest of heart-essences.
They are the heart of hearts,
The heart of the Dharma.

It does not appear to be real.
It fulfills all the accoutrements of our lust.
Our apparel is a blazing light.
It appears and it withdraws.
It encompasses the place where we are.
This is not some other place.
It is the place of the heart.
It is difficult to teach.
The Rishis of old who were meditators
Also did not get this.

Lack of desire,
The absence of an object of desire,
And a basis for desire:
These are said to be holy.
There is nothing more to be explained.

Any description we may make
Is a hope to exemplify the Buddha,
And is a great delusion.
Delusion and the path of enlightenment
Are just ideas.
They are not things that we may acquire.

It is not possible
That one who desires to achieve high status,
As it is,
Will find it.

Dharmas do not come to exist
From out of thusness.
Dharmas that exist are not to be found.

They are embodiments of ideas.
There is no essential objectivity to them.
They are beyond philosophical theories.

Obsessing about practice is an obstacle to freedom.
The desire to be freed through a search
Is the work of children.
The true Dharma of the All Good One is great.

The twelve branches of causes and conditions
Is a group that is not to be practiced.
It does not go anywhere.
It does not stay anywhere.

Self-aware wisdom is our own mind.
It is the best.

Even if we are butchers and prostitutes,
Or we have done inexpiable things,
Nothing will obstruct us,
For we understand self-awareness.

As things are,
The doers of evil are the finest community.

There is nothing to learn or to study,
So there is nothing to be written out.

The entire dominion of the Dharma
Is contained within this great bliss,
For it is magnificent and spacious.

These spacious skies are not free from birds.
Wisdom does not depend on method.
There are no atoms that do not move,
Just as they are.
There is no failure in our objective.

Those who follow along the trails
Of the practices of the Rishi meditators
Cling to conventional words for their highest views.
They take hold of something,
Saying: "It is,"

And engage in the objective they are seeking.

This Dharma is not to be taught
By saying: "This."
This is primordial Buddhahood.

The teachings about holy things
Have no essence.
I grant empowerment into the way
Of the lord who has created all things.[57]

There is nothing to be related,
So there is nothing to be written out.

To have meaning or not to have meaning,
To be happy or not to be happy:
These are entirely absent here.
This is why we must not meditate.

We settle into the way it is,
Just as it is,
Just as it is with a circle:
Without thinking,
Without disturbance,
Without a view,
And without a meditation.

In the same way that oxen who are tortured by thirst
Do not change,
Even though they drink,
It will not come to pass
That a heart of self-awareness
Will come to us from someone else,
For we ourselves,
Just as we are,
Abide without changing,
And our wisdom shines
In the midst of all the Buddhas.

Be free from practicing communities.
Be free from trails of thought.

---

[57] Kun byas dbang phyug

This is the best of the best:
The embodiment of a glowing heart.

We do not desire Buddhahood.
We do not desire to be Tathagatas.
We do not use words for practice.
We have no writings.

If Vajrasattva were not shining from above,
We would not find the meaning that there is
In written teachings.

There is no object to think about.
It is inappropriate to visualize anything.
There is no path of success.
There is no end to the functions of words.

We will not see our objective
By working on doors and studying levels.
Our limitations will not be removed
Through the practice of the three samadhis.
We will not find our objective
By working toward something that is a result.

In the same way that everything comes to us naturally
From a wish-fulfilling tree.
Everything occurs to us naturally
When we are in this excellent place.

Those who desire the meditations of the Rishis
Must not seek for them.
To dwell in an unspoken equanimity,
And have no mantra words of any kind to recite:
This is the best form of recitation.
To have nothing whatsoever to contemplate,
That is our meditation.

This heart-essence of excellence
Is a place for everyone.
It is not a thought.
It is not an attainment.
We place ourselves in the way it is,
Just as it is.

Then Vajradhara asked:

Blessed One,
Unchanging Light,[58]
What is the meaning of this Tantra?

The Blessed One entered the equanimity of the samadhi of praising the Tantra, and he intentionally spoke on this topic:

Primordial equanimity:
This is the spaciousness of the circle.
Not to depend on anything
Is the essence of a circle.

The Victorious One,
The Buddha himself,
Is correct.
Not to think about anything at all:
This is a heart of excellence.

This is spacious and vast.
Its inner depth is deep.
It is inappropriate that anyone measure it,
Even a little.

This is the sky.
No one can estimate it.
It is beyond having a body or a voice,
And there is nothing to designate as being a mind.

This is certain.
There is nothing to be taught
By saying: "This."
There is nothing to be contrived
By saying: "This is primordial Buddhahood."

Just as a magnificent garuda soars through the sky
On the trackless pathways of the birds,
This king of the effortless transmission
Is astounding to us all.

---

[58] 'od mi 'gyur ba

Do not contrive to study it.
From the beginning,
We have needed nothing whatsoever
For our supreme result,
For we are primordially Buddhas.

From A Razor for the Lotus and a Sword for the Wheel,[59] the King of Tantras on the Heart-Essence that is the Origin of All Things,[60] the Magnificently Embellished Tantra,[61] The King of All the Tantras,[62] this is chapter twenty-six: The Contents of the Tantra.

It is finished.

This was translated by the Indian preceptor Śrī Singha and the Tibetan translator Vairochana.

---

[59] sPu gri pad ma ral gri 'khor lo
[60] Kun 'byung snying po rgyud kyi rgyal po
[61] rGyas pa chen po'i rgyud
[62] rGyud thams can kyi rgyal po

THE NATURAL INTENT OF THE SECRET HEART

In the Indian language:

Vajra Guhyagarbha Satva Mahākhabhyertha Tantra

In the Tibetan language:

rDo rje sems dpa' nam mkha' che

gSang ba'i snying po rnal ma don gyi rgyud

In the English language:

The Tantra on the Natural Intent of the Secret Heart

Of Vajrasattva's Magnificent Sky

THE BASIC SCENE

I bow to the glorious Vajrasattva!

I will explain this in words, for once.

The Blessed One,
Being by his very nature the great perfection,
A spontaneously formed wisdom,
A king of self-arising awareness,
A circle of clear light,
Great bliss,
Was in the palace of awareness
That does not pass away or change,
In a single company that had no divisions
With the Buddhas of the three times,
The sentient beings of the three realms,
And those who have views about the path.

Then Vajra of Awareness addressed the Tathagata King of Awareness with these words:

E Ma'o!
The secret of all contemplations
Is a state of emptiness, peace, and compassion.
This is the most excellent magnificence of a heart of hearts.

Please speak well
On the meaning of the great perfection.

Then the Tathagata King of Awareness spoke on the significance of the great circle that is not to be sought out:

The sphere of the self-arising secret circle
Subsumes every Dharma,
With none excepted.

We succeed spontaneously,
Without travelling and without seeking.
This is not something that we acquire through study.
It is a space of perfection.

The king of awareness is totally luminescent.
He is the one who perfects
Everything that we may desire.

The path to total freedom
Is an ocean of wisdom.
It perfects all the vehicles,
And is spacious like the sky.

Self-awareness is a true heart of goodness.
The dominion of the Dharma is the true nature of all things.
It is empty of exaggerations and denigrations.
It is one.
It absolutely does not have parts.
We gather everything into a single vehicle.
Uncorrupted wisdom is pure.

The self-arising circle of the sun rises up.
Its great pervasion is the embodiment of the Dharma.
Great emptiness is the seal of awareness.
It is pure from the beginning,
And it will not be left behind.

Secret wisdom is the Bodhicitta.
It is identical to the magnificent sky.
The great circle is a primordial teaching.
We live in a dominion that does not expand or contract.
There is no object for us to visualize
That we might exaggerate or depreciate.

The clarity of self-awareness
Has no center or border.
It is the true nature of everything.
It is secret.
This is why it is empty
With respect to objects,
Things that ideas and analytics can hold onto.

One who dwells in the equanimity of undistracted awareness
Does not contemplate the teachings on the wheel of samadhi.
In a contemplation that comes to him by itself,
Everything is perfect.
Spontaneous success without a search
Is something that comes from ourselves.

The Mahamudra dwells in the self.[63]
The seal of awareness has no substance.
It is a state of non-meditation
That cannot be left behind.
This is the blazing light of a heart of wisdom.
It abides in the self,
For it is the heart of everyone.
It is, in fact, a self-nature
That is difficult to plumb or measure.

We are perfected in the heart of the one vehicle.
It perfects all Dharmas,
For it lives in our spirits.
It remains there naturally,
In the circle where all our intentions are fully perfected.
It has no stages.

An awareness of the heart
Is the Tantra that is meaningful.
This Tantra is the quintessence of our vehicle.
The seal of wisdom is supreme perfection.
We do not leave it behind.
It brings an end to all the applications of our consciousness
That concern themselves with what there is.

---

[63] bDag, Atman

A mind that has no cause will have no conditions,
So how would it be born or end?
We are finished from the beginning,
So there is nothing to do.
We are perfected spontaneously,
So we have nothing to contemplate.
We are perfected through ourselves,
So we have nothing to work on.
The significance of non-visualization
Is not something to meditate on.
We are perfected in a single instant,
So we have nowhere to travel toward.

The seal of the awareness of wisdom
Is perfection in the total fruition of our liberation.
The secret word of self-originating awareness
Is not to be spoken.
We know it by its meaning.
This is something that abides in unity.
To look for differences is a path of delusion.

The heart of this
Is the perfection of the mind itself.
It is not something that was created by our memories,
Our senses, or our attitudes.
We live in what happiness there is,
Without avoiding it or working on it.

So he spoke.

From the Tantra on the Natural Intent of the Heart this is chapter
one: The Basic Scene.

PLANTING THE TRANSMISSION
OF SPONTANEOUS SUCCESS
WITHOUT A SEARCH

Then again the Blessed One, the Tathagata, the King of Unsought Awareness entered into the equanimity of the samadhi of spontaneous success, and proclaimed these words:

The dominion of the Dharma is not to be sought.
We succeed spontaneously, without a search.
Effortless non-seeking is the way that it is,
From the beginning.
This self-originating secret dominion is unspeakable.
It is beyond the objects that we define, clarify, and process.
It cannot be distinguished from
A pure awareness of the three times.

Awareness is an indivisible union
That is perfected spontaneously.
We do not accumulate
A space for primordial Buddhahood.
It is not to be learned.
There is nothing to think of or say
About the space of endless awareness.

Everything has been perfect since the primordial.
The true self is spontaneously perfected.
We do not travel over any levels.
We do not study on any path.

157

To study samadhi without understanding it
Is the disease of illusion.
To settle into our unsought self-nature
Is success.
When we enter this space without distraction,
That is meditation.
When our awareness is perfected in unity,
That is a gathering.
When our self-nature does not join to anything,
That is samaya.
When we succeed spontaneously, without a search,
That is fruition.

To maintain that a duality
Comes from out of a state of non-duality
Is an obstruction for the circle.
When we hold that the one circle is dual
We are fettered by ideas.

There is one truth,
But we make attributions about it
That are based on erroneous transmissions.

There is a unity that we cannot think of,
But we use false ideas as references
To think about it.
We gather up causes and conditions
To signify self-origination.
We look at the impure as being pure,
Making disturbances for the pure.
We are chained by the mudra of conceptualization,
And we destroy the mudra of wisdom.

Unspoken wisdom is the supreme proclamation.
It is ruined when we speak of it.
Through meditating on a mandala of definitions
We reject the mandala of wisdom.
Through meditation on equanimity and emptiness
We lose the mudra of great bliss.
Through craving for definitions and words
We fall into extreme views.

Supreme bliss does not distinguish
Anything at all.
It plays in its dominion.
The heart of hearts is the wisdom of awareness.
The meaning of meanings
Is when the meaning of everything
Touches our minds.
The Tantra of Tantras
Connects all things
In a natural perfection.

The transmission of effortless perfection
Is stamped with the seal of great bliss,
Primordially.

This is not something that can be left behind.
It is luminous in its spontaneous realization.
The self-originating is one,
It is self-apparent,
But is looked at in nine ways.
The play of this spontaneously-realized form
Is most amazing.

Its true nature is one,
Yet it is complete in every virtue.
Through letting things be, without seeking them,
All our virtues are completed naturally.
In the result that happens by itself,
Spontaneously made without assembly,
There is nothing but awareness.
From the primordial,
We are perfected spontaneously.
We do not get this through study.
It is a purity that is represented symbolically.

This is a freedom from visualizations,
Pervasive like the sky.
We will not find the wisdom of awareness
By saying words
About the inconceivable, unspeakable dominion of the Dharma.

When the seal of great bliss
Is stamped upon our settling into non-searching,

Everything will clearly be
The mudra of the supreme bliss of wisdom.
This is not emptiness.
It is not non-emptiness.
It is the middle.

What this is
Is what it is.
There is no self or other at all.
All our thoughts are exhausted.

We have no consciousness of union.
The dominion of supreme bliss
Is empty and self-luminous.
It is self-aware.
It conforms to the dominions of the three seals.
It is not possible to leave it behind.

In the dominion of the three embodiments,
We are not without the recognition of symbols.
They are brilliantly obvious,
Are not disturbed,
And are not obstructed.
Our undisturbed nature is luminescent.
This is Buddhahood.

The wheel of being undisturbed
Cuts through obstructions.
When we think about being disturbed or undisturbed,
We are not disturbed.
We do not use the four times
To separate the undisturbed from the disturbed.
We recognize the measure of the time,
According to our instructions,
As great bliss.

When both disturbance and non-disturbance are clear,
It is certain that we will succeed in our holy contemplations
Spontaneously,
Even though we do not apprehend
The clarity and luminescence of a disturbance.

The three evils are the same,
With respect to happiness,
So we have no fear of samsara.
We experience this success spontaneously,
So we have no hopes or fears regarding a result.
In the miracle of awareness,
There is no need to seek, practice, or work.

So he spoke.

From the Tantra on the Heart's Intent,[64] this is chapter two:
Planting the Transmission of Spontaneous Success Without a Search.

---

[64] sNying po don gyi rgyud

PUBLISHING THE THREE TRANSMISSIONS WITHOUT CONTRIVANCE

Then again the Blessed One, the King of Awareness dwelt in the samadhi of publishing everything, and proclaimed these words:

Kye!
O yogins of this great assembly,
Our own minds are perfect.
They are naturally clear.
The unspeakable is not published
Using grammar, logic, and proofs.
The essential meaning of the unspeakable
Is exemplified by proving
That our awareness is not contrived.

We must understand awareness experientially,
Just as we experience the wetness of water.
If we do not have the experience
To understand how things are,
Then no matter what words or symbols for words
We may talk about,
We will be following after ideas
About the doors of the symbols.
We will lose the truth,
And be bound in the irons of conceptualization.

There are no dharmas that are not pervaded
By the circle of self-originating awareness.

It does not expand or contract.

In this dimension we are perfected.
The transmission of the vajra
Of the awareness of great bliss
Is obvious in itself,
Without our contriving it.

We settle this into this.
When we are settled
We will succeed spontaneously,
Without exertion.

We succeed spontaneously,
Without a search.
As an analogy,
This resembles the light of the sun.

The true nature of the uncontrived mind,
And the proofs about the way it is with awareness,
Are not what this is,
And are not anything else.
Non-dual awareness is perfected in a single moment.

The great bliss of total perfection
Is neither wide nor narrow.
The heart of our own mind's spontaneous realization
Resembles the awareness of an experience.
In which we have no awareness of any clear light
Of any kind.
We perfect our self-awareness within our own dominion.

The transmissions that use magical words for their methods
Exemplify spontaneous success without a search,
Even though the great bliss of self-originating clear light
Does not move from its non-dual intent.

This is a method for understanding everything.
However things seem,
Apply them toward the intent of happiness.
This is a teaching on a method of discipline
From among the oceans of practices
That accommodate our engagements.

To differentiate between gradual and instantaneous
Is to divide a single entity,
Based on great and small particularities in our ideas.
In the significance of non-duality,
They are obviously one.

The bountiful vehicles that are methods of discipline
Are one
In the heart-essence of the self-originating vehicle.
Self-originating awareness is not an accommodation.

An ocean of teachings
Is perfected in our hearts.
This is real,
But if it is not methodically exemplified,
Then even though we are pervaded by a single self-origination,
We are like the children of kings that wander around.
We do not understand our own characteristics.

So it is that while our true nature is one,
We use the power of our thinking
To divide it into separations.
We use symbolic instructions that are connected to meanings
To understand the mudra of the unspeakable mind,
And just as soon as we are sure of the meaning
We are so fortunate as to be liberated without any effort.

We do not leave the meaning of great bliss behind.
We enter the path of the mind
Without looking for it,
And it takes us to the end.

This is not gradual, but instantaneous.
Our awareness is perfected in the effulgence of the mind.
We succeed spontaneously, without a search.
We have no position or preference.
This position-less self-origination is pervasively clear.

Without cause,
And without conditions,
The Bodhicitta is spontaneously perfected
Without our gathering up anything.

It is perfected in a single moment.
Self-originating light encompasses us pervasively.
Its blessings of compassion do not come or go.

According to the perfected transmission
Of the one vehicle,
Which is our own mind,
Everything without exception is stainless and completely pure.

We are done with all our work,
Nothing excepted.
We succeed spontaneously.

This is not contrived.
It is not to be sought.
We succeed spontaneously.
Our thoughts do not dwell on emptiness or applications,
So they are empty.

The things that corrupt the transmission of liberation
Come from placing ourselves where there is no peace.
They are the fetters we make by looking for ideas.

Movement is not to be associated with the mind of awareness.
We abide by a method in which we do not search,
And we do not practice.
Nothing can disturb this.
We go where we please.

This does not expand.
It does not contract.
It fills in vacant areas.
We will understand it by settling ourselves,
Without meditating,
As we dissipate.

Do not think!
Do not practice!
Do not seek any object!
This is the cause!

The unattached Bodhicitta is not a contrivance.
This Tantra on the Heart's Intent[65]
Cuts through our conceptions about clarity and non-clarity,
The holy and the ordinary.

So he spoke.

From the Tantra on the Heart's Intent, this is chapter three:
Publishing the Three Transmissions without Contrivance.

---

[65] sNying po don gyi rgyud

TEACHING THE METHODS
BY WHICH THE BODHICITTA
IS TO BE UNDERSTOOD
AND THE WAY TO UNDERSTAND IT

Then the Blessed One, the King of Self-Originating Awareness,
entered the equanimity of luminous purity, and proclaimed these words:

The Bodhicitta is not static,
By its very nature.
The three-hundred-sixty false understandings
Turn out to be ways of making something existent
Out of non-existence,
And continue to be vehicles
For the world of our cravings.

The Bodhicitta is not generated.
It does not end.
It is like the sky.
It does not depend on anything.
It is beyond ideas and practices.
It has been proclaimed to be
The vehicle of uncontrived perfection.

The ten scriptures[66] that have been published
Clearly teach that there is one true nature.
This is the core of three transmissions,

---

[66] Lung bcu

Brought together.
It is a secret treasure that joins all the tridents.

Mind is self-originating.
It pervades space.
It is not a dharma that is to be divided up.
It is through the special qualities of playfulness
That the teaching that the mind is, in itself, nine spaces
Has been promulgated.

The transmission of the view of self-originating perfection
Brings everything together,
With nothing left out.
All things are perfected in a single circle,
And they play within a single self-originating heart.
The secret circle is a dominion for all things.
It remains natural,
Without border or end.

The secret in all things
Is self-originating sentience.
Self-awareness is devoid of non-awareness.
We abandon the consciousness
That awareness is an idea or an application.

The transmission of the treasure of the samadhi of awareness
Plays in a dominion
Where there are no hopes or fears.
Self-awareness does not contemplate the dominion of an object.
The emptiness of the All Good is not contrived,
So all the specifics on the methods of the All Good
Are perfected in clarity,
Without confusion.

For this reason they are like
The planets and the stars arrayed in the sky.
All things are perfected in a single circle,
So the ten great resolves
Of being without tasks or searches
Are not to be sought out in any ten true natures.
That would be like a universal monarch holding onto land.

A most excellent prince, a fortunate one,
Who is taught this methodically
Will understand it.

We use three resolves for an uncontrived method
To bring things together into luminous wisdom.
Everything is subsumed within the three realities.[67]
This will set the meanings of the symbols free.

Everything is just the mind.
However we may divide up the special qualities of playfulness,
As we encounter and do away with views,
We remain in the reverted city of non-understanding.

The benefit of self-originating perfection
Is that it is a magnificent method
That requires no search or practice
By which we touch upon a contemplation
That cannot be disturbed.
We join together the ways
That the three lineages are exemplified.
This is the true nature of uncontrived perfection.

For so long as ideas are our cause
This will be beyond our comprehension.
I am teaching this in conformity with the powers of thoughts.
This is something you must know well.

Our unsought true nature is spontaneously realized.
Total perfection is primordially encompassing.
It is well known that it is astounding.

We are perfected in one moment,
Without contrivance and without study.
Any search for some thing that occurs to our intellect
Is, in fact, a search for a spontaneously realized true nature
That has not been contrived.
Anyone who uses the magical key of awareness
To open the door of the mandala of self-originating methods,
Will see the great bliss there is
In spontaneously realized self-origination that is not contrived.

---

[67] De nyid gsum

We do not join with or part from this treasure of awareness
In any of the three times.
It is spontaneously realized, without contrivance.
It is not to be sought.
We discontinue our consciousness for visualizing things,
So we are not disturbed.

There is a single self-origination,
But its manifestations are countless.
We abide in a circle of non-duality,
So we have nowhere to travel toward.
The welfare of living beings is clear in our minds,
So we are finished with what has already been done.
Everything is perfected spontaneously,
So we do not work toward any fruition.
The unborn is entirely pure,
So we do not clear away obstructions.
The effortless is perfect by its very nature,
So we are free from any good works.

When we understand only this,
We accomplish everything.
Everything is perfect.

This is what is described to be
Living in the unity of the circle of the great perfection.

So he spoke.

From the Tantra on the Heart's Intent, this is chapter four:
Teaching the Methods by which the Bodhicitta is to be Understood, and
the Way to Understand It.

SELF-ORIGINATING PERFECTION

Then again the Blessed One, the King of Self-Originating Awareness, entered the equanimity of the samadhi of great bliss, and proclaimed these words:

Great bliss is a heart of luminous self-awareness.
Everything, with no exceptions, is perfected
In the state of non-duality.
The heart of hearts
Is the path of natural emptiness.
Great bliss tastes like the end of the sky.
This is the best of hearts.
We live within its intent perfectly
When we understand
That unborn clear light is bliss itself.

Supreme bliss will not fit into the domain of the sky!
It is vast!
It is great!
The state of the circle is to be one.
It has one essence,
But there are bountiful ways to understand it.
The special characteristics of our result
Have been proclaimed to be beyond reckoning.

The heart-essence of the unborn
Is a dominion that is not to be exaggerated or denigrated.
In the heart-essence of the unborn
We see Buddhas and sentient beings.

We do not see the heart-essence.
We see the perfected mind itself.
There is nothing that reaches the end,
For nothing is written down in this dominion.

The significance of this self-originating great bliss
Is especially noble.
Those who delight in grammar, speech, and words
Do not understand what this means.

The heart of hearts does not visualize
Any thought or statement.
Not thinking and thinking are not a duality.
They have a single end.
They do not dwell in any center or extreme,
So they are not to be examined or conceptualized.

We abide in the way things are,
Without understanding and without thinking.
Self-awareness that is not conceptualized
Is great bliss.

Without seeking it,
We abide in the dominion of awareness.
The true circle of the secret of great bliss
Continues,
In a way in which it pervades the sky.

The heart of the unborn
Is the Bodhicitta.
It dwells in a state that cannot be joined or parted from.
We place ourselves in the heart of self-originating enlightenment,
A natural state that we do not seek,
And we do not work on anything.

Something may be in a state of wisdom,
But to the face of our thoughts
It will be wrong.
An optical illusion may be taken to be water
By our intellects,
While in reality,
There is nothing to put down or take up.
The consciousness that makes attributions is inconceivable.

The true nature of the Bodhicitta
Is that awareness and everything there is
Are there at the same time.
They are there,
Without any stages.
So it is that they are a great bliss.

An uncontrived heart is the supreme intent.
It is well known to be an excellence
That is self-originating and is not to be sought.

The mind of awareness blazes by itself,
Without our seeking it,
Without any consciousness of some shining butter lamp.
We use the way of the unmoving to discriminate it.

The Mahamudra accommodates everything.
Ideas about definitions will not move it.
We are primordially stable
Within the wheel of our own natures.
A mandala of awareness
Is not something we generate.

The home of blazing wisdom
Is adorned with the luminosity
Of unobstructed self-origination.
The three times are the Victorious One's own nature.

All our intentions are perfected
In the state of non-duality.
The King of Self-Originating Awareness
Has no consciousness of awareness
That has its origin in memory.

All our mantras, mudras, offerings,
Our austere practices and our great deeds
Will, without our seeking it,
Become a mountain of reversions that binds us.

What shall we do?

We give up all our tasks,
With no exceptions.
We do not act.
We do not seek.
We do not hold onto anything.
We come into our own nature,
Which is without consciousness.
We settle into self-originating bliss.
We are free.

Understand this by placing yourself into your own nature,
Without seeking it.
It is a secret space
That is not some emptiness that we have contrived.
We accustom ourselves to engaging with
The objects of our awareness.

An ordinary mind is an equanimity
That has no happiness.
It is, of itself, the flavor of great bliss.
The clear light of wisdom is great bliss.

Everything, with no exceptions, is just the mind.
It is stainless.
When the mind itself,
It being naturally pure,
Is in balance with the way things are,
Without our seeking it,
It is stamped with the seal
Of self-originating great bliss.
Awareness illuminates its objects without moving.

When the mind of the Mahayana
Is itself perfected,
There is no need to refer to
A path where we traverse over levels.

This is not to be sought.
We accomplish it spontaneously.
It is not to be worked toward.
It is primordial Buddhahood.

So he spoke.

From the Tantra on the Heart's Intent, this is chapter five: Self-Originating Perfection.

WORKING WITH THE MUDRA OF GREAT BLISS

Then again the Tathagata, the King of Self-Originating Awareness, made his own true nature totally clear. He proclaimed these words:

The ancestor of the ancestors
Of all the Victorious Ones of the three times
Is the King of Awareness,
The self-originating Bodhicitta.

The mind is, itself, a spontaneously perfected great bliss.
It is perfection itself.
I myself am the Victorious Ones of the three times,
The perfect Buddhas.

When we engage ourselves in the uncontrived Bodhicitta,
We do not see.
We are not free.
We are stuck in samsara's mud.

Those who place themselves in this spontaneous realization
Without seeking it
Are the fortunate children of the Victorious Ones.
They are my heart.

So he spoke.

Then the Bodhisattva Vajra of Awareness asked:

Kye!
The true nature of the Victorious Ones of the three times
Is physical, verbal, and mental.
This is a teaching of the King of Self-Originating Awareness,
Which is you.

Your heart is one.
It is self-originating wisdom.
What do you think about this topic of contemplation?

So he spoke.

The great King of Awareness proclaimed his response:

This mudra of supreme bliss
Is the true nature of everything.
Everything is subsumed within
The state of this contemplation.
It leaves nothing out.

Do not dwell in a consciousness that thinks and practices!
Everything is pervasively illuminated
By self-originating light.
The heart-essence that is the true nature of everything
Subsumes all things.

The great secret is not contrived.
Pacify your exaggerations and depreciations.
They are not this true nature.
This is beyond all definitions.

This is not a true self.[68]
It is spontaneously perfected.
It is the heart-essence of everything.
It is not anything at all.
The heart-essence of non-existence exists!

By virtue of the natural perfection of effortlessness,
Compassion arises,
Like the light of the sun,
Without our seeking it.

---

[68] bDag nyid

All the vehicles are perfected
In a single self-origination.
So the soul[69] that perfects all meanings
Through understanding one word
Dwells in supreme bliss,
Just as it is,
Without doing anything,
And without remaining still.

When we place ourselves in our own nature,
Without seeking,
Our thoughts will be exhausted.
If we live by a method
In which we are not disturbed
Our chains will be broken.

According to the significance of natural purity,
The dominion of the Dharma,
Which has no boundary or center,
No outside or inside,
Is not to be meditated upon.

We let things fade away,
Without being disturbed,
Becoming accustomed to our own nature.

The mudra of playfulness is one.
It cannot be stopped.
Emotional problems are the self-luminescence of wisdom.
They are not to be rejected or worked on.

Do not traverse a pathway!
Do not study on a level!
It is not possible to leave behind
The state of spontaneously realized wisdom.
If fulfills the wishes of all the kings,
Who are equal to the sky.

All things, with no exceptions,
Are a single circle,

---

[69] bDag, Atman

And we are perfected in its dominion.
The way this is
Is unborn,
Does not stop,
And does not seek.

This is the heart-essence of the supreme vehicle.
It perfects everything.
Our natures are spontaneously perfected
Without our doing anything.

This is beyond ideas and practices.
We use all things as objects for our play.
We will not understand
The uncontrived heart-essence of the Bodhicitta
When we are using an awareness
That follows the trails of signs and conventionalities.

We throw away the things we crave,
And the things we analyze,
So we are not chained by a dualistic understanding
Of non-duality.
We place ourselves in our own nature,
Without any contemplation,
And our obstructions are cleared away.

From the beginning,
We are cleansed of darkness,
So there is no need to clean anything.
This is realized spontaneously,
So we do not request it from another person.
It is perfected in ourselves.
It is not to be denied.
It is not to be travelled over.
We dwell in our own nature,
Without effort.
This itself is perfection.

We do not contemplate, seek for, or work on any deeds.
We do not divide virtue from evil.
We are primordially without stain.
There is no fault
In the total union

That comes from practicing the methods of desirelessness.

The domain of the Victorious One is astounding.
The heart-essence of self-originating luminosity
Perfects all things.
Nothing whatever stops it.
It works to train living beings.

Whatever way our own nature may be
Is the way in which we live.
Clear light is not in a duality
With the self-originating mind.

All our searches for a practice and a meditation
Are delusions.
We succeed spontaneously
In the practice that we do,
Without seeking to.
When we understand this heart-essence
Of self-originating perfection,
We will never speak of "being obstructed"
Or "not being obstructed."

From the Tantra on the Heart's Intent, this is chapter six: Working with the Mudra of Great Bliss.

EMPOWERMENT
INTO THE EFFULGENCE OF AWARENESS

Then again the Blessed One, the King of Awareness, spoke out on the so-called "effortless natural perfection."

The mind itself is self-originating.
I have transmitted the empowerment well.
Everyone has received the empowerment
For the pervasive space of self-origination.

The empowerment of great bliss,
The spontaneously perfected king of goodness,
Does not depend on receiving an empowerment.

The space of empowerment
Is the perfection of our own minds,
So that they are luminous in complete perfection.
It does not depend on an empowerment
Into the mandala of a mudra.

In the state of this unspeakable heart,
Everything is perfect,
So I do not refer to an empowerment
Into the bliss of the words in a mantra.

Beyond all definition,
Our minds are perfect.
So we do not seek for meaning

In implements or in samadhi.

The great empowerment
Of the Brahmanic vase of royal investiture
Is not granted.
We are perfected by our own natures.
When we understand this,
We will live in a bliss we achieve spontaneously.
This is the supreme empowerment.

The King of Awareness
Grants empowerment to everyone.
Do not contrive to depend upon
Empowerments that are conceptually defined.

When we understand
The supreme empowerment of empowerments,
The empowerment of profound perfection,
We will be spontaneously perfected,
Without being imparted anything.

This is primordial Buddhahood.
It is not a compounded thing.
It is an empowerment without birth or ending.
It is not to be traversed gradually.
It is an empowerment of perfection in a single instant.

We do not need to understand it
To succeed.
We are perfected in our own nature,
Which is what we have been from the beginning.

The meaning of perfection,
In the circle of our own nature,
Is beyond speech,
But it is exemplified as being a delightful wisdom.

It is a luminous wisdom.
It is our indivisible true nature.
It is not to be visualized.
It is a wisdom that has no definition.
There is nothing that transcends spontaneous realization.

The seal is stamped.
Receive the four empowerments
Of uncontrived spontaneous perfection
In the empowerment into the effulgence of awareness
With happiness!

Awareness that is received through searching,
And instructions that are received through time,
Are methods of acquisition used by unfortunate transmissions.
We use a method in which we place ourselves
In a self-originating condition,
As is appropriate.

A magical mirror of jewels
Is displayed in the mind.
Meditate well in your heart
On the instructions from the aural transmission.
They are bound with the sign of a seal.
Keep them well, for the duration.

So he spoke.

From the Tantra of the Heart's Intent, this is chapter seven:
Empowerment into the Effulgence of Awareness.

PRACTICING MAGNIFICENT METHODS

Then again the Blessed One, the King of Unseeking Awareness, proclaimed this chapter on practicing magnificent methods:

Yogins who have entered the space of wisdom
Teach people who have investigated the orations,
And who keep to the mudra,
The supreme bliss of self-originating awareness,
Which is a mental ease.

They open the door with a sign,
Which is a key of jewels.
When they penetrate well
The three awarenesses,
Which are the samaya for awareness,
And are not to be protected,
They will be serious about not transgressing.

They will receive all the empowerments
Of supreme bliss,
Which is spontaneously perfect by its own nature.
The one who is spontaneously perfected through his understanding
Has proclaimed this.

He has opened the door
To the treasure of awareness
That is in the three transmissions.

The interpretable transmissions
Are to seek and not to seek.
In the transmission of what is sure,
We will understand
The transmission in which ideas are, in fact, the mind.
These arise uninterruptedly
From what self-originating clarity is.

Our path of practice
Is obviously anything that is, in fact,
Great bliss.
We do not travel over any path.
We do not study on any level.
We live spontaneously,
In the self-originating perfection
Of our hearts.

The heart-essence of all dharmas
Is one.
It is the Bodhicitta.
It does not exist in numbers, divisions, or differences.

Because the aural transmission
Is a true method for understanding these things well,
We will get an excellent liberation
Through being instructed in its significance.

We roll the root into one,
And examine it evenly.
We will understand the true meaning
Through dividing it up,
But the meaning of a good understanding
Is that we stay in the one.

So he spoke.

From the Tantra of the Heart's Intent, this is chapter eight:
Practicing Magnificent Methods.

THE SUPREMACY
OF UNTREMBLING AWARENESS

Then again the Blessed One, the King of Self-Originating
Awareness, said that there are no dharmas that transcend non-duality:

> For all the Victorious Ones of the three times,
> The true samaya for awareness
> That settles into itself
> Is primordially perfected
> In our nature of self-originating perfection.
>
> We live in this nature,
> But if we do not have the bond
> Of self-originating perfection,
> We will not get beyond the deviant pathway
> Of samaya that are defined.
>
> The three samaya of perfection
> Are to engage in what we like
> Without being disturbed.
>
> All the bounteous samaya
> That the Victorious Ones of the three times
> Use to train living beings,
> By means of the door of speech,
> Are, according to the meaning that we do understand,
> No more than one.

This is not a contrivance.
It is a transmission of settling into ourselves.
There are no dharmas
That are not stamped with the seal:
The three natures[70] and the one circle,[71]
So no one whosoever exists who transgresses them.

In the samaya of the unerring heart
We use a memory of undisturbed clarity
To go to the end of clarity.

The mind that experiences great bliss
Teaches the mandala of the mind.
The true mandala of awareness,
Which is the source of all things,
Will not become totally perfect in the future.
It is a subject that is not to be left behind.
It must be taught well.

What is apprehended by the mind
Does not change through the three times.
The vajra samaya is a transmission of signs.
Use the words of the instructions
To understand this clearly.

According to the samaya
Of spontaneously perfected great bliss,
We live naturally,
Within an untrembling understanding
Of what is meaningful.

When we use exemplifications
Of the meaning and nature of this,
And use the samaya of grammatical definitions
For the uncontrived and for our contemplation
It will not be possible for us
To get beyond our personal objectives.

---

[70] Rang bzhin gsum. These are the three natures as presented in Yogacara philosophy.
[71] Thig le

The true heart of the holy ones
Is a perfect contemplation
Of self-originating awareness.

As it is with the true nature
Of water and the ocean:
They are indivisible,
Vastly diffuse,
And well-known to be astounding,
The transmission of a perfected heart
In a single moment
Is a self-originating unity.

It has no differences.
There is nothing that surpasses this.
It is completely perfect.
This is the samaya of unsought spontaneous perfection.
It is stamped with the seal of the wisdom mudra.

There are no stages.
This is self-originating primordial Buddhahood.

So he spoke.

From the Tantra of the Heart's Intent, this is chapter nine: The
Supremacy of Untrembling Awareness.

SETTLING INTO HAPPINESS
WITHOUT TRAVELLING

Then again the Blessed One, the Tathagata King of Awareness,
spoke on what it means not to study or travel.

The true nature of the Bodhicitta
Has no stages that may be applied
As causes and conditions.
It is by force of the attributions made by false ideas
That we calculate numbers
For an incalculable intent.

In the search for something other than
The one that does not travel,
We travel.
We look at something that has no stages
In terms of stages.
Where there is a single heart-essence,
We use our ways of seeing
To develop an inconceivable number
Of ways to travel on a path.

There is a single heart-essence,
But no matter where we travel
We will not find the meaning
Of travel-free perfection there.

The total perfection
Of the pervasive dominion of the Dharma
Has no edge or border.
It is perfected in an instant.

Awareness that does not travel
Is spontaneously perfected.
Without seeking any enumeration of ideas
About the five paths and the ten levels,
We realize our own self-natures spontaneously.

The vehicles of seeking
Are reverted Dharmas.
Perfection in one instant
Has no stages.

We live forever in self-luminous light.
There is nothing to meditate on
As a form for our samadhi.

Our results are achieved spontaneously
Within ourselves.
So when we divide the Buddha from sentient beings
We are empty.

No one travels on the path of the self-originating heart,
But we are, instantaneously,
In a place of perfection.
This resembles the way in which
The sky encompasses everything
Without travelling.

The Mahayana is a path
In which the mind itself is perfect.
There are no Dharmas,
With no exceptions,
That it does not encompass.
The result that we do not travel towards
Is natural perfection.

There are no paths.
There are no stages.
The path of the mind

Is not a conception.
The mind of clarity
Has no thought or action.
It is just like entering a river.

With the three characteristics,
Which are the true natures of all things,
The three embodiments are perfected in a single moment.
This is why we do not work on
Gathering accumulations and cleansing away obstructions.

From the beginning,
The great perfection is the Bodhicitta.
The mind of effortless awareness
Is engaged in its spontaneously realized nature.

A mind that is totally undisturbed
Is a path
For a stainless pure mind.
We do not travel on it.
It is primordial Buddhahood.

So he spoke.

From the Tantra on the Heart's Intent, this is chapter ten: Settling into Happiness without Travelling.

PLACING AWARENESS INTO HAPPINESS

Then again the Blessed One, the King of Self-Origination, spoke
on the meaning of the secret awareness of the spontaneously realized vajra:

All Dharmas are one in the Bodhicitta.
The mind is, of itself,
An even clear light.
To settle down like this,
Without disturbance,
Into a spontaneously manifest domain,
Is the best.

To encounter the meaning
Of self-originating perfection,
We settle into our uncontrived true nature
At the very instant there is an object for our awareness,
And we stay that way.

The undisturbed river of awareness
That settles into itself
Shines with memory,
And has a pattern.
The heart-essence of equanimous self-awareness
Is not contrived.
Engage in what you like!

An untroubled intellect shines with clarity.
We understand it by its motion.
It is evident by its clarity.

We melt into its dominion,
And we blaze in light.

The heart of wisdom
Combines the brilliant and the corrupt.
The circle melts into an absence of any true nature.
We dwell in the clear mind
Of the wisdom of awareness,
Which we realize spontaneously,
Without a search.

We do not use our minds to make obstructions,
And we also let our bodies and our voices
Settle into dissipation.

Give it up!
Let it be!
The Bodhicitta is beyond visualization.
Live naturally!

The intellect that does not change
Through the three times
Is engaged in a space of perfect wisdom.
The total purity of the three resolves of the awareness
Is uncontrived,
Just as it is.

The secret mind
That we do not join or part from
Shines in this dominion.

The awareness that is the source of memory
Is perfected in this dominion.
We place our own minds,
As they appear without our prejudices,
Into whatever we enjoy,
And we do not move.

The wisdom of self-awareness is inconceivable.
We engage in a dominion
Where there is no consciousness.

Everything is perfect,
Without any acquisition or rejection,
So there is absolutely nothing
To hold onto as a definition,
Great or small.

The intellect that puts the three times into one
Abides in the mind's true nature,
Without our seeking it.

Use the mind of the equanimity of great bliss
To see!

From the Tantra on the Heart's Intent this is chapter eleven:
Placing Awareness into Happiness.

ASSIGNING THIS
TO THE FAMILY OF THE MAHAYANA

Then the King of Self-Originating Awareness spoke on the
instructions for the king of vehicles:

E Ma'o!
This is the heart-essence
Of the bodies, speech, and minds,
Of all the Buddhas.

If we prioritize wealth and fame,
And use our failing minds to promulgate it
Among the perverse people of the world:
Those who have no faith or samaya,
Who are poor in wisdom, compassion, and Bodhicitta,
And poor in the five requisites for holiness,
Who are small in study,
Who are arrogant,
Who have little respect,
Who have great avarice,
Who are lost in factions and unholy things,
Who cling to their positions,
Believing in them and reflecting on them,
Who prioritize fame in the world,
Who reject the possibility of enduring purpose,
Who work for fame and to make others afraid,
Who have not received the words of instruction
In the aural transmission,

Who explain the secrets falsely,
Who do not have the resolve of the wisdom of awareness,
The objects that we see will demolish us,
And at the instant we fall down,
We will be lost from the family of the free.

All those who keep the faith and samaya,
Who possess faultless virtue,
Who are immersed in the significance of the Mahayana,
Who serve the Dharma and their guru,
Who do not look out for their bodies or their lives
When they would please their Vajra Guru,
Who are supported by the seven precious things,
Who have little lust for material things,
Who are not impoverished,
Who are ascertained to be in the secret family of the Mahayana:
We must open the door of secrets for them.

These are the words of the holy ones.
If we bestow the secret significance on
Those who do not give away their precious things immediately,
Do not have an attitude of service to the holy ones,
And have failed to be Vajra Gurus,
The only place for us to go
Will be the vajra hell.
We will be held to our commitments,
Just as we have made them.

So he spoke.

From the Tantra on the Heart's Intent, this is chapter twelve:
Assigning this to the Family of the Mahayana.

The Tantra of the Natural Intent of the Heart of Vajrasattva's
Magnificent Sky[72] is finished.

---

[72] rDo rje sems dpa' nam mkha' che snying po rnal ma don gyi rgyud

THE TIBETAN TEXTS

THE TANTRA OF GREAT BLISS

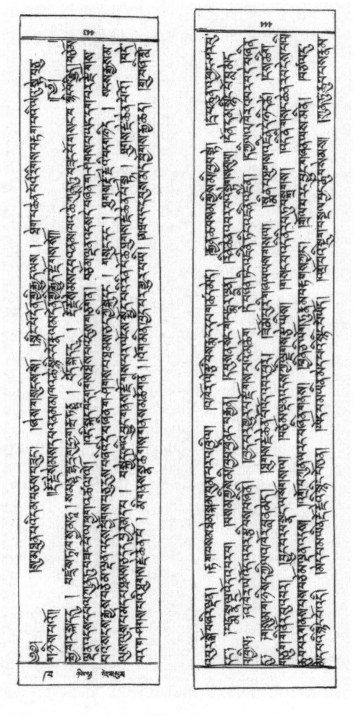

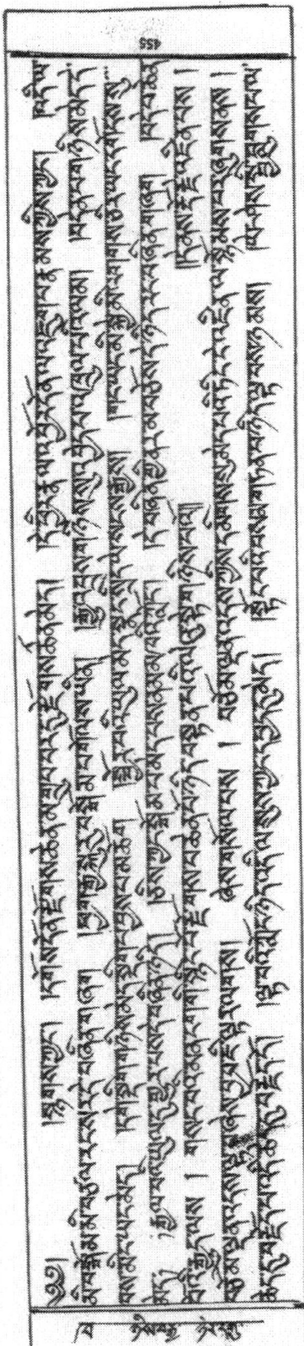

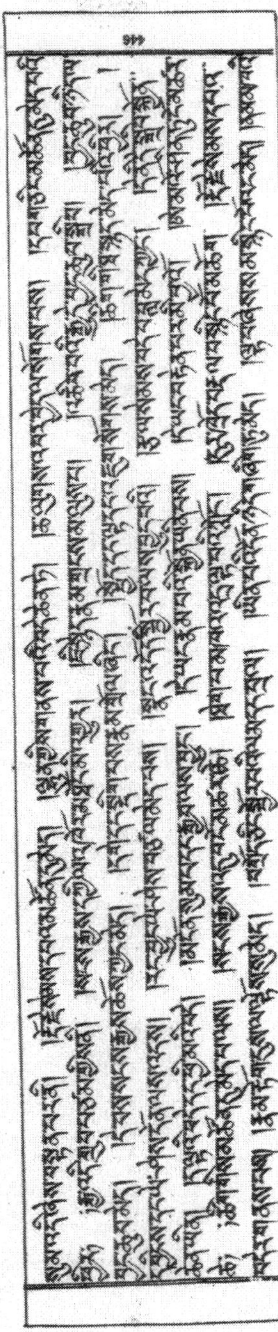

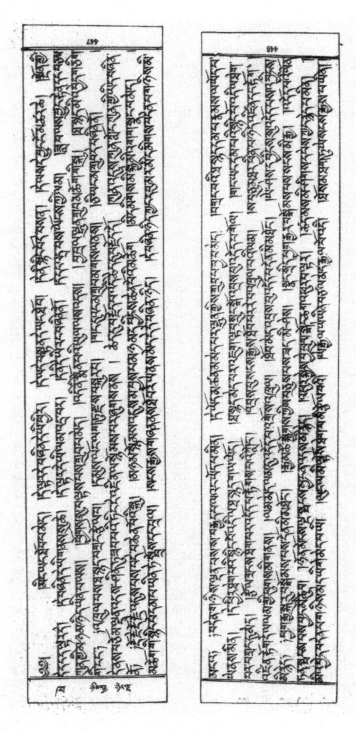

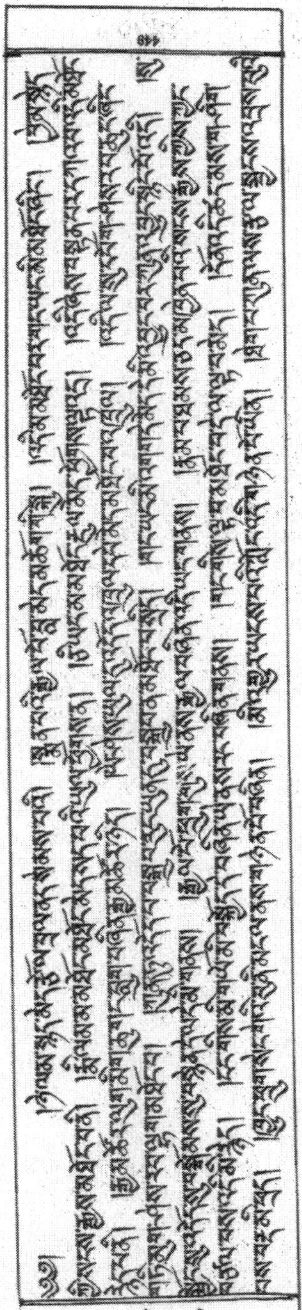

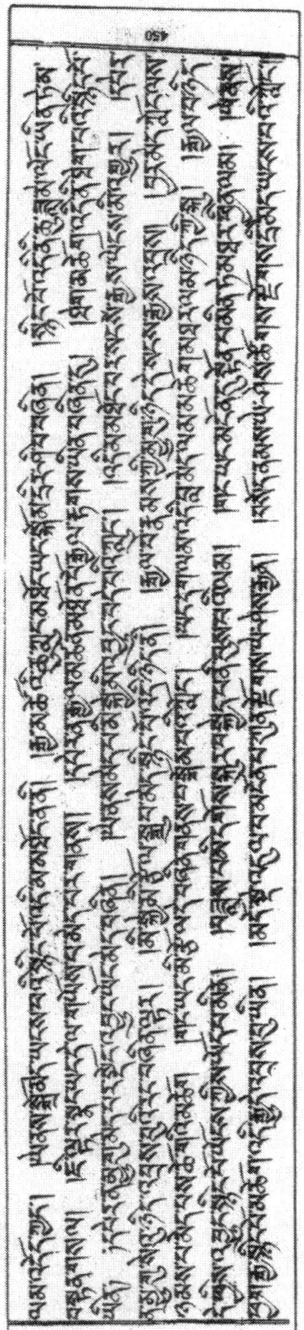

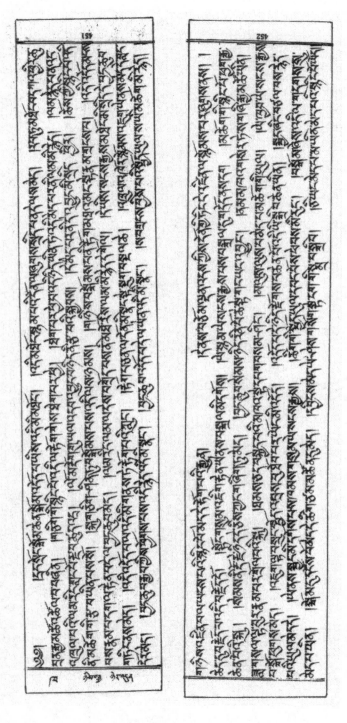

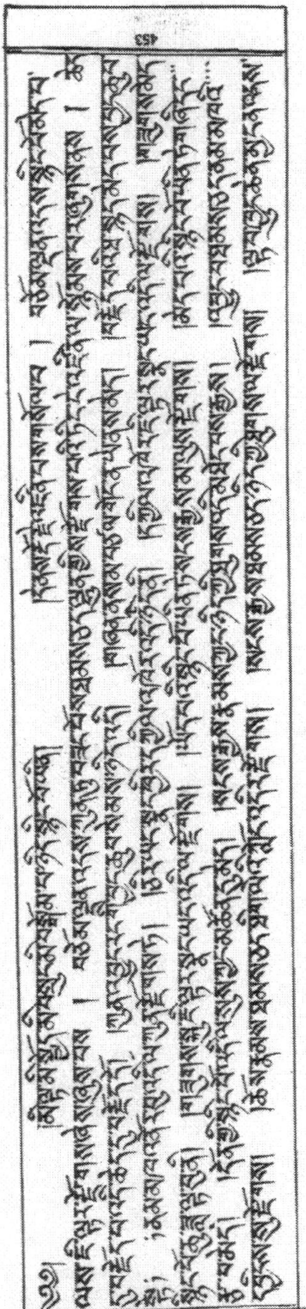

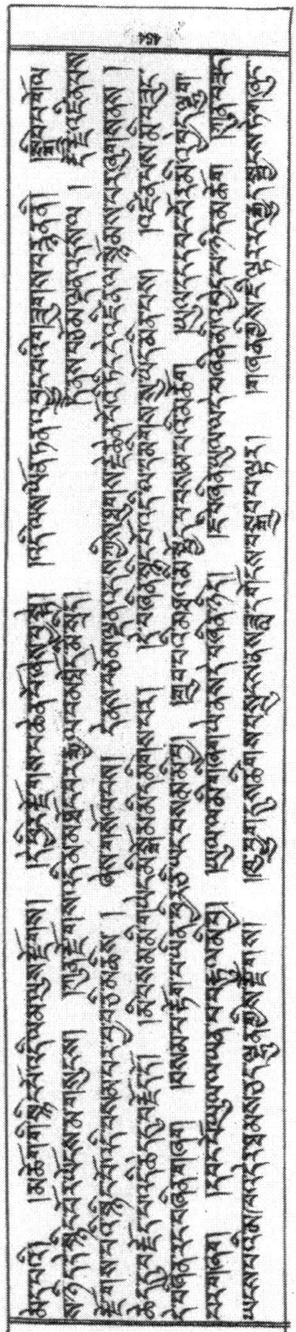

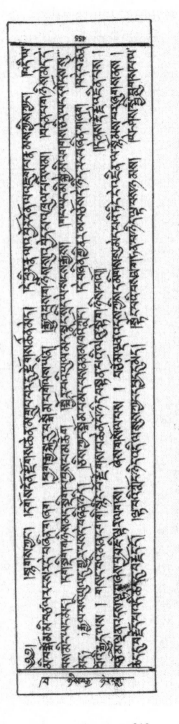

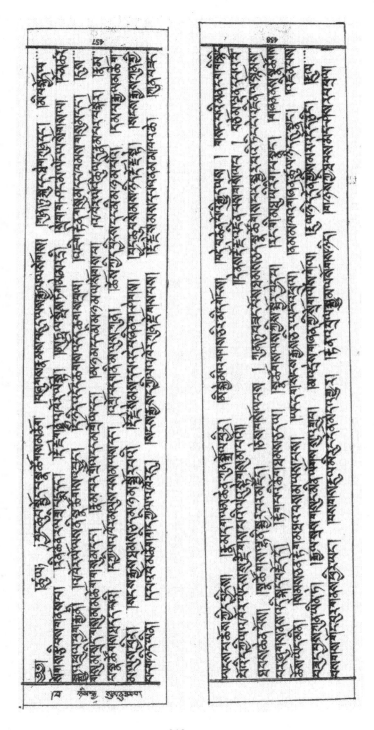

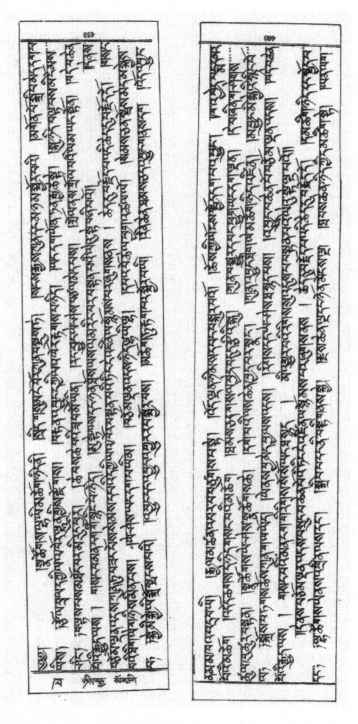

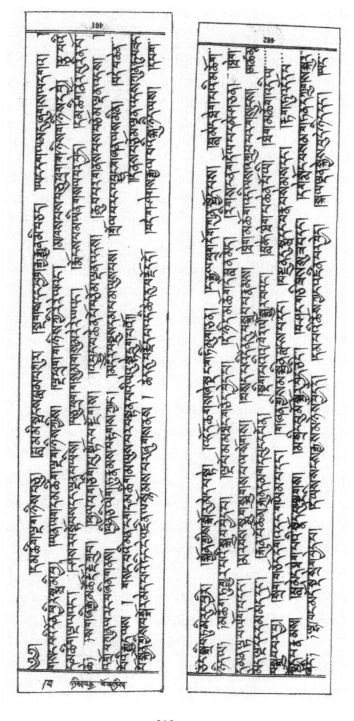

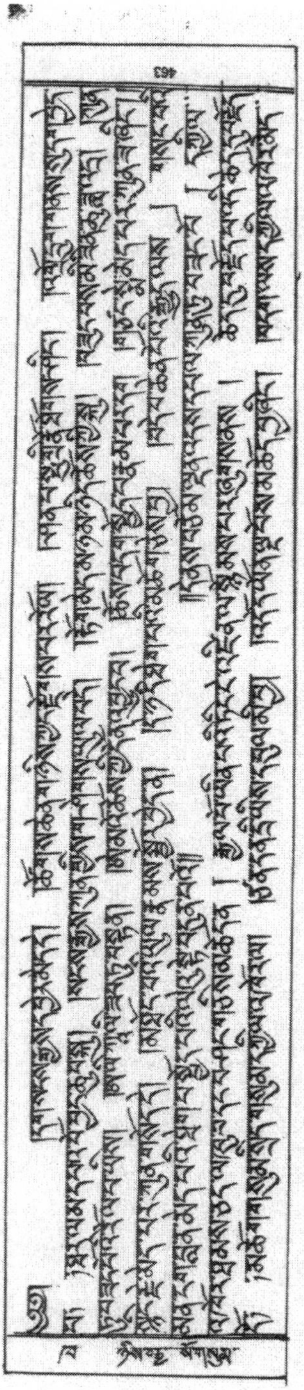

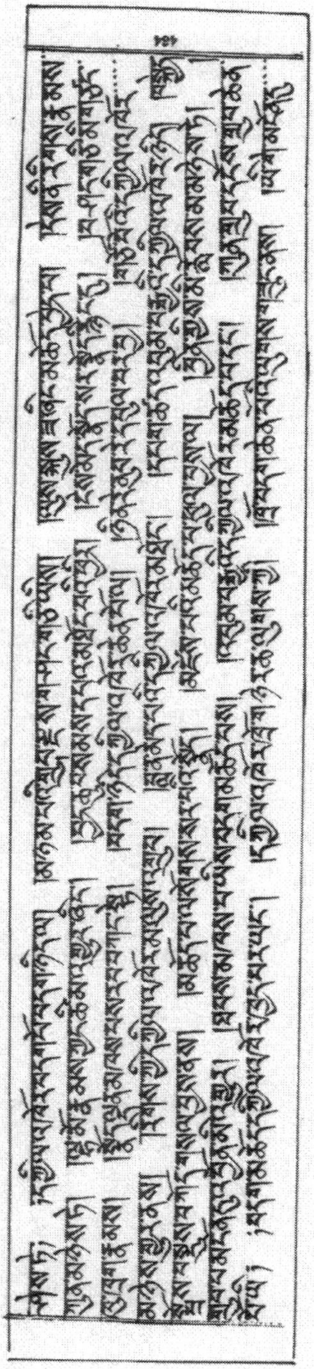

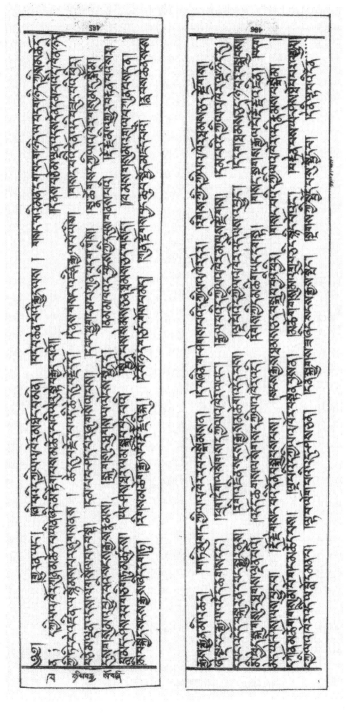

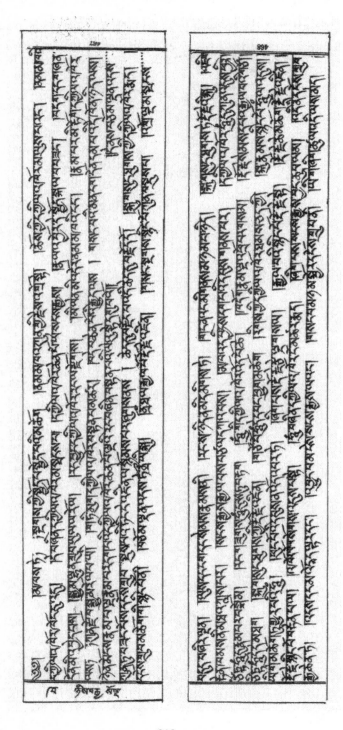

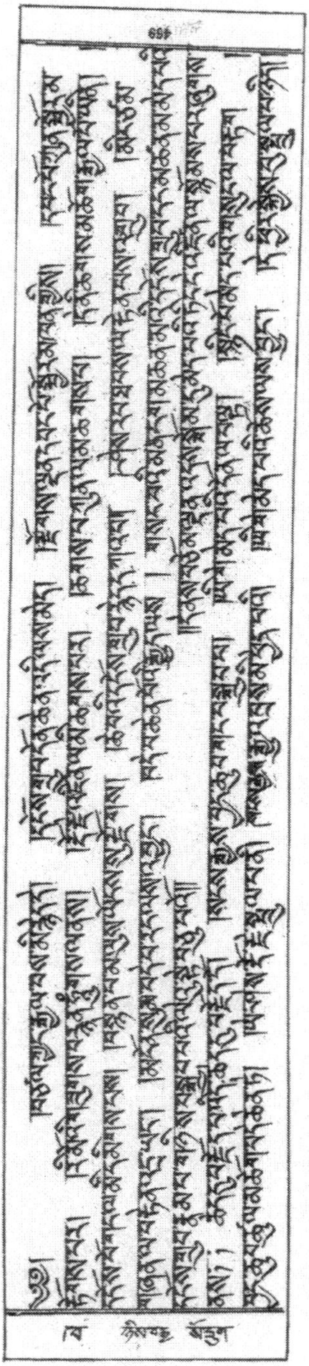

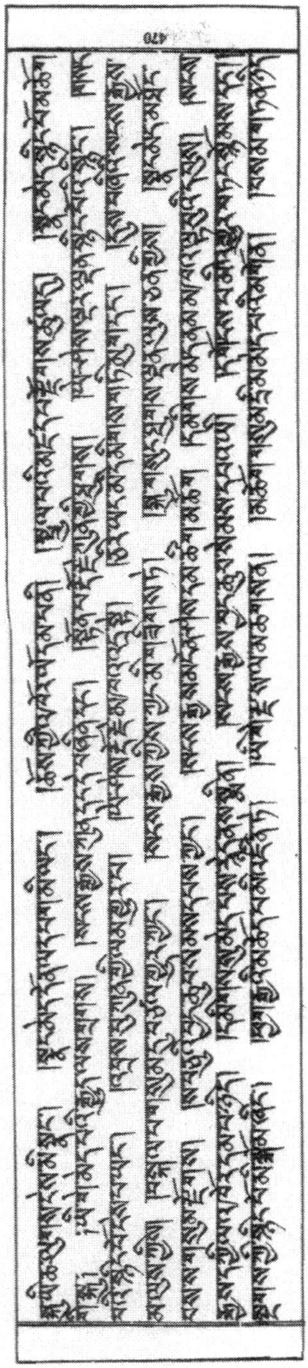

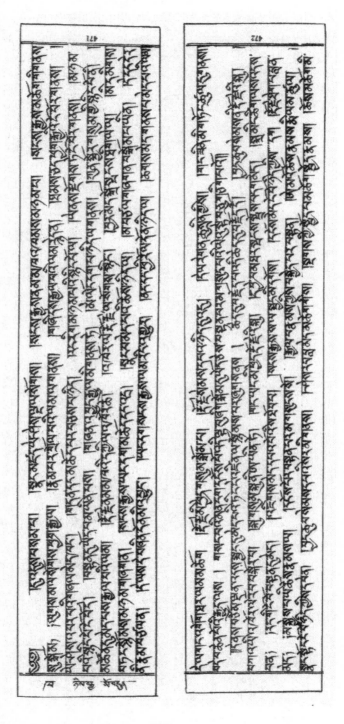

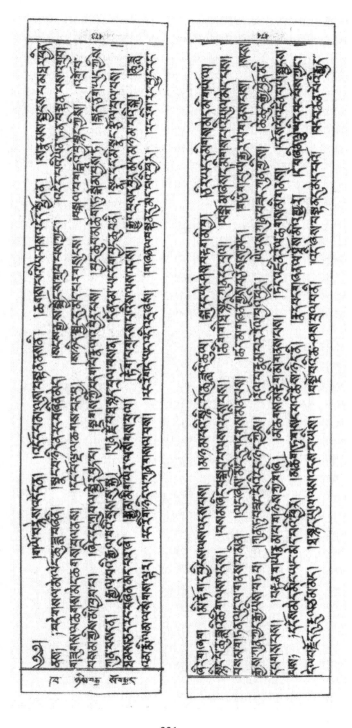

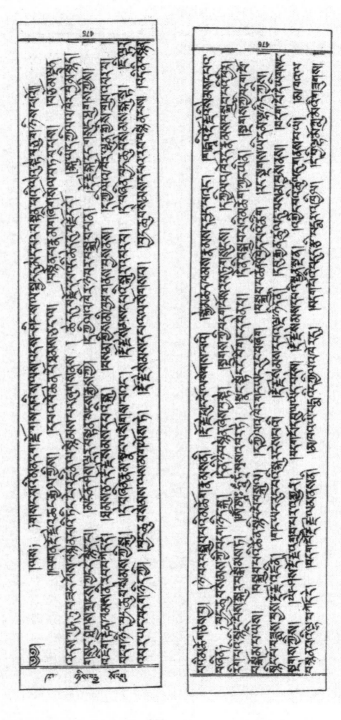

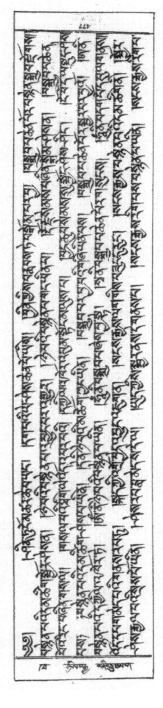
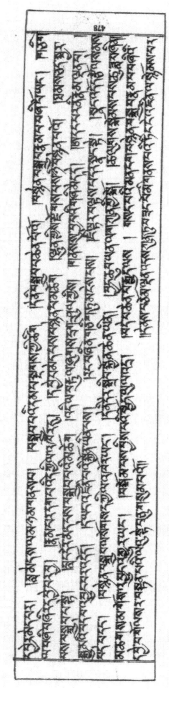

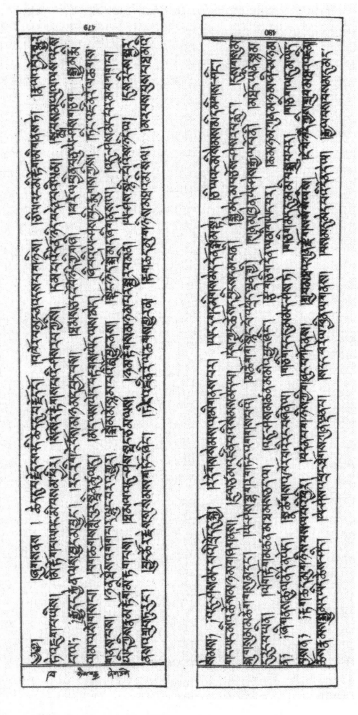

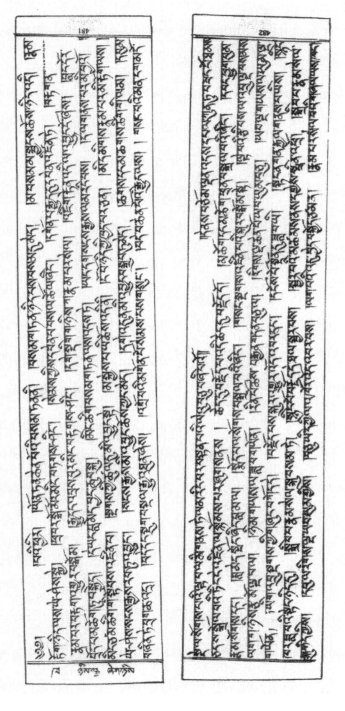

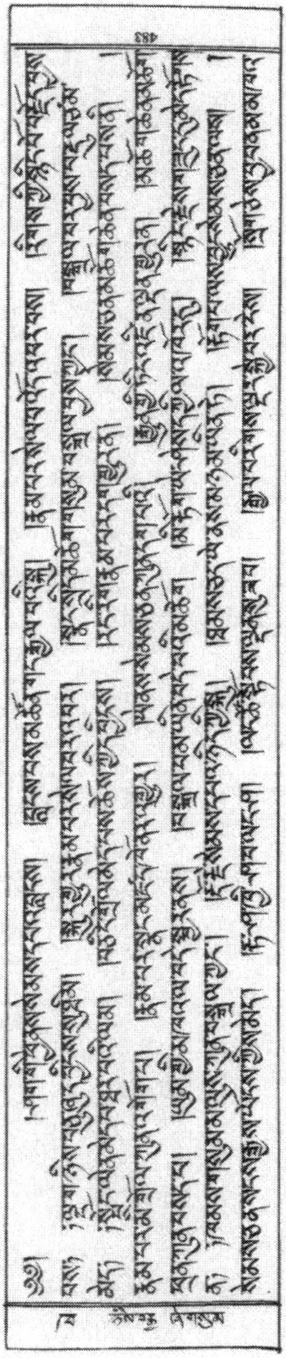

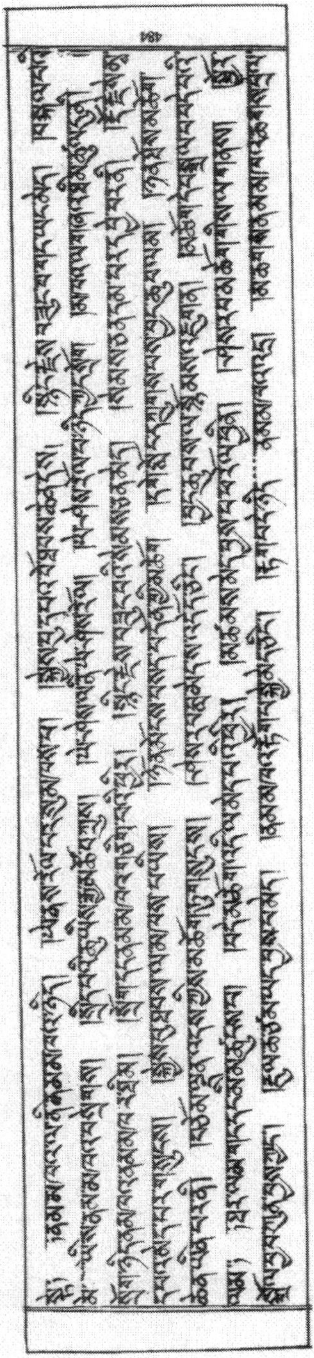

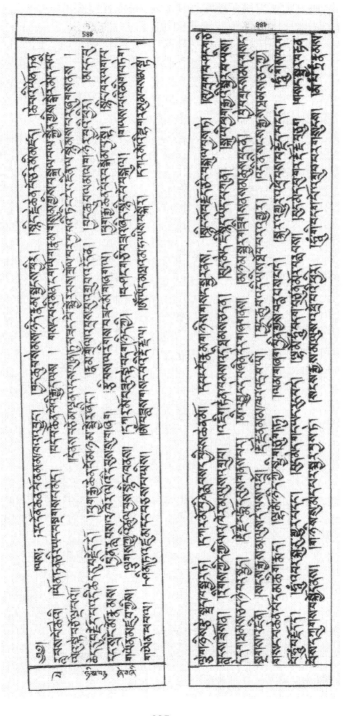

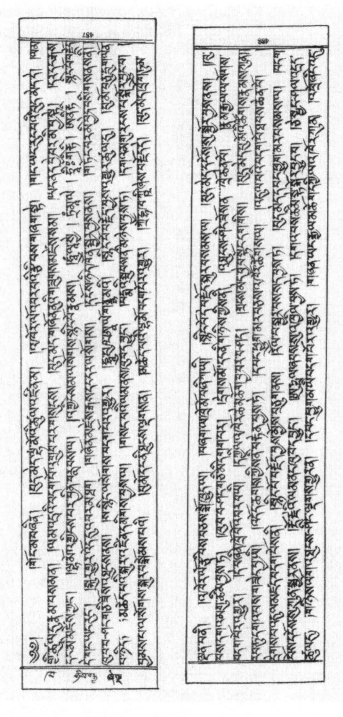

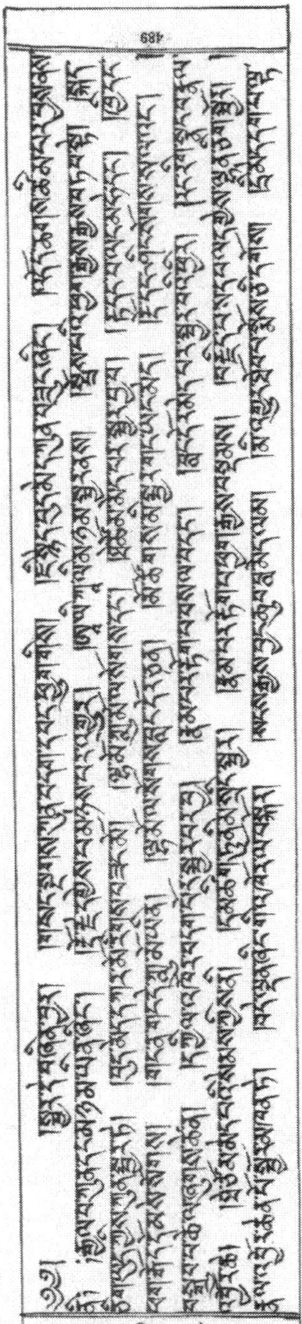

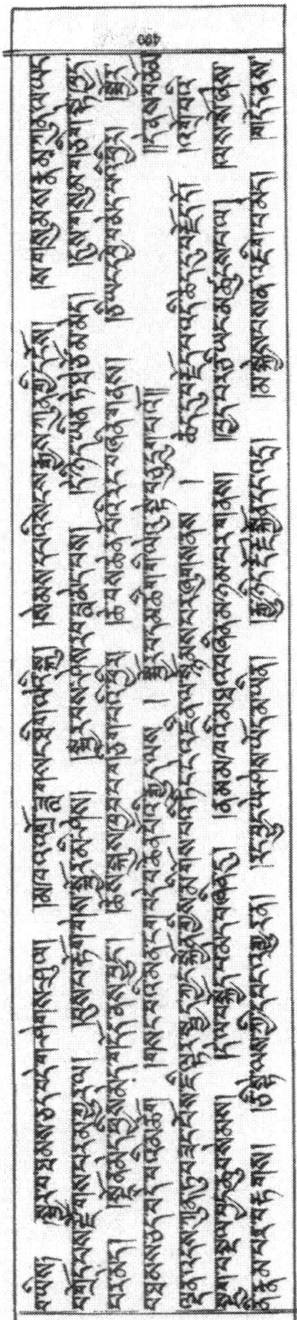

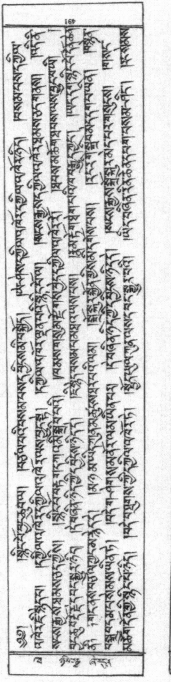

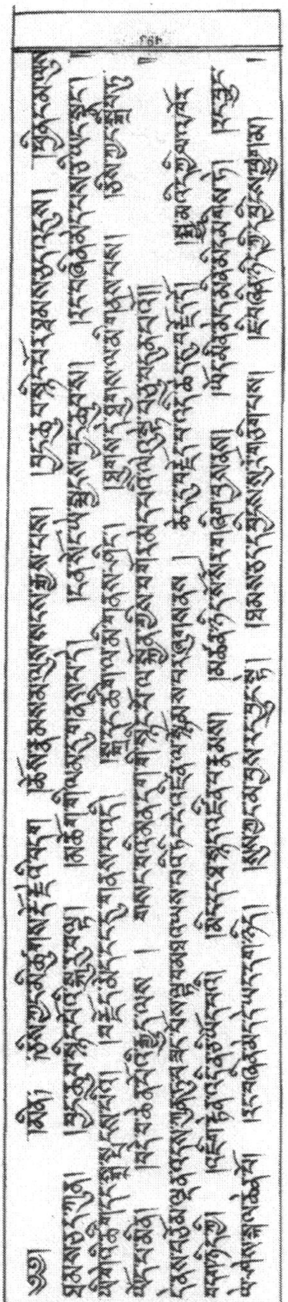

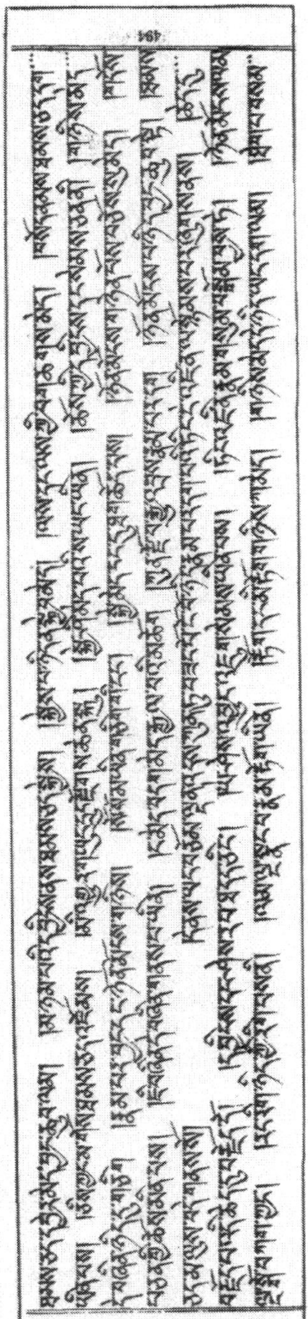

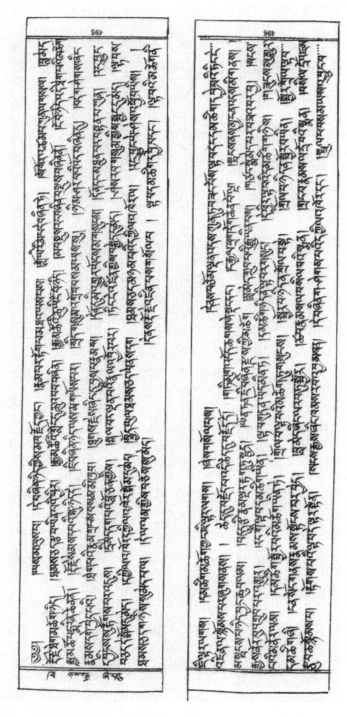

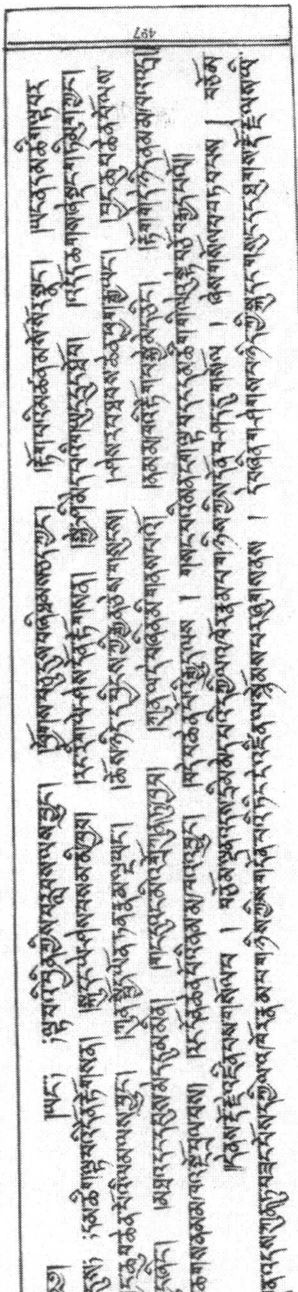

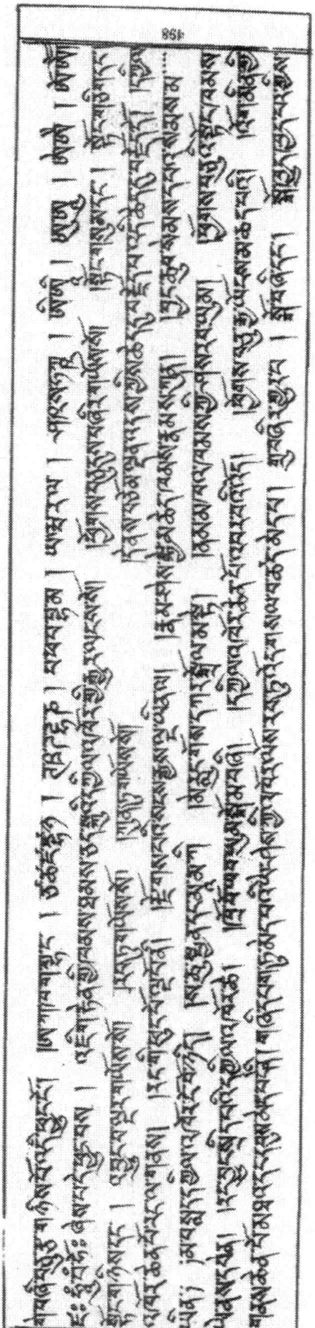

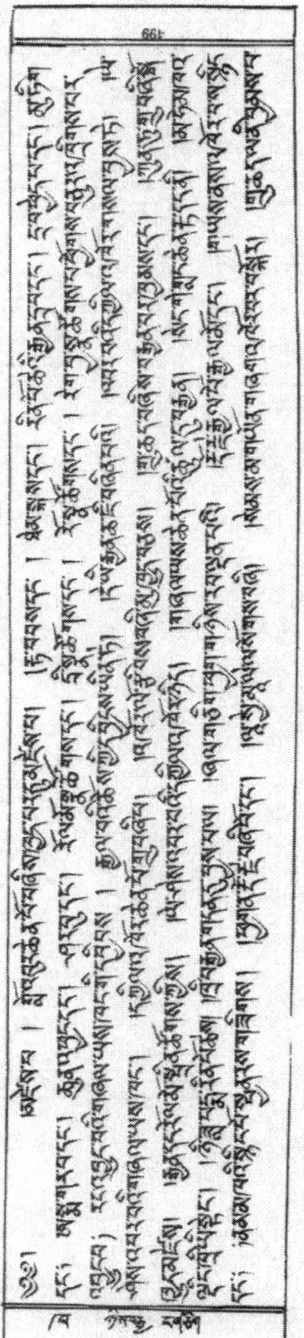

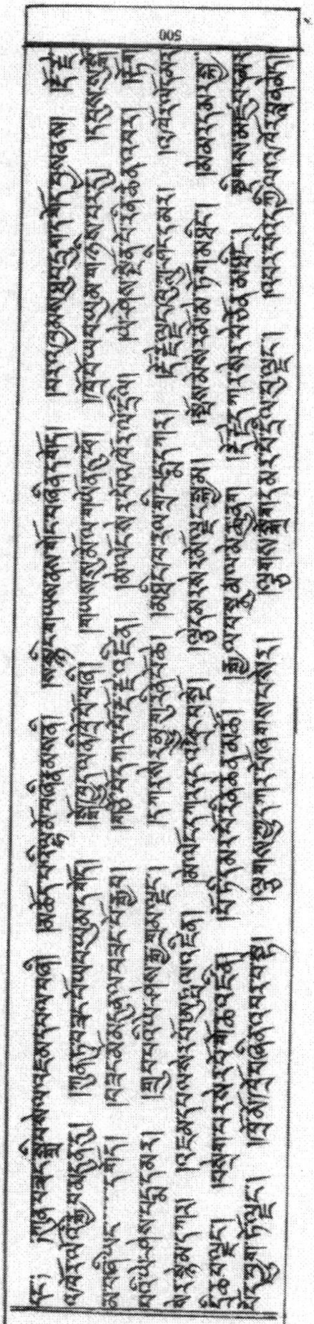

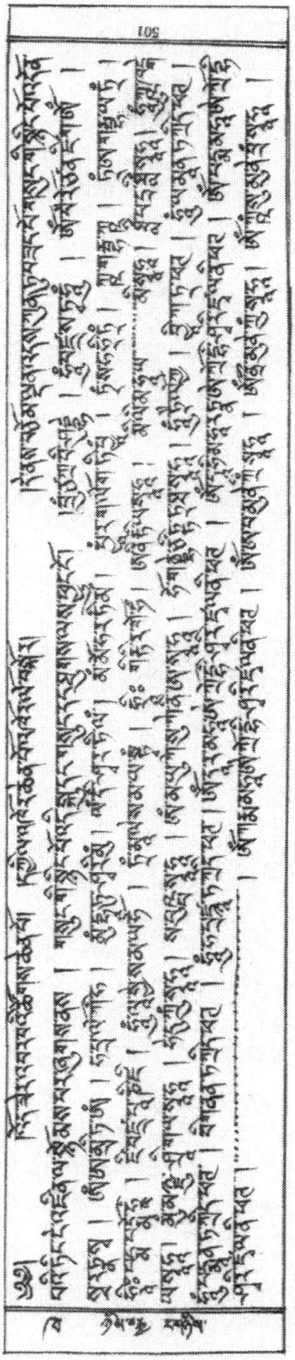

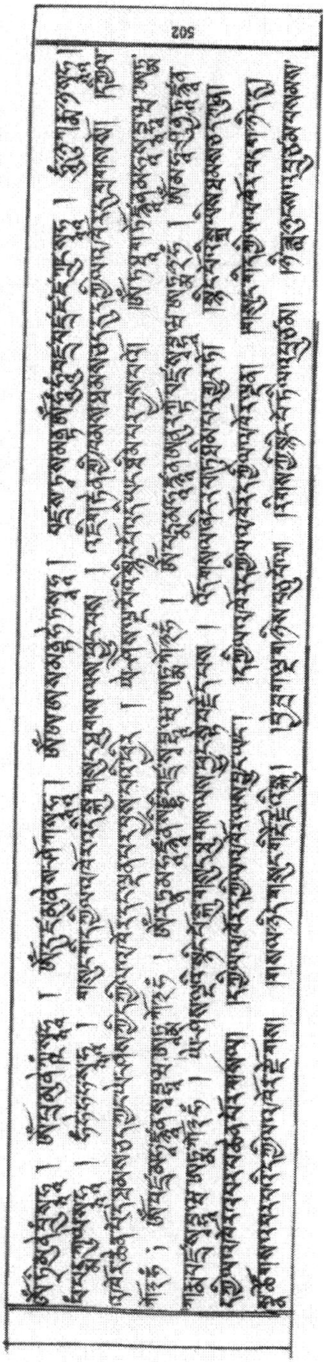

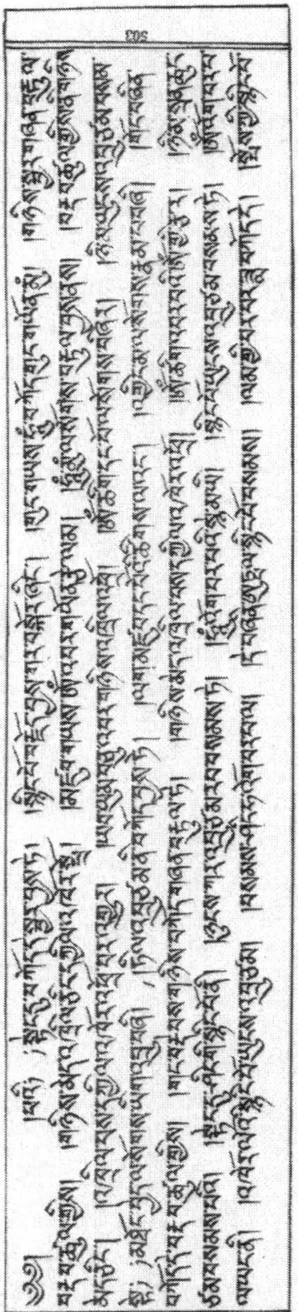

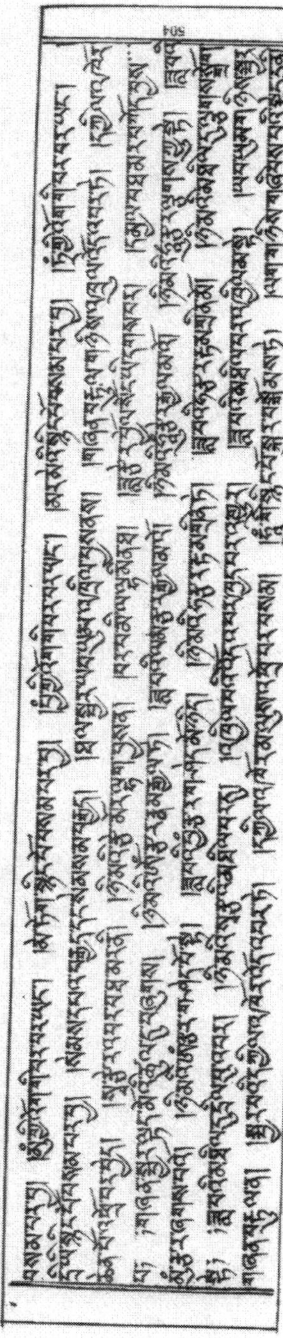

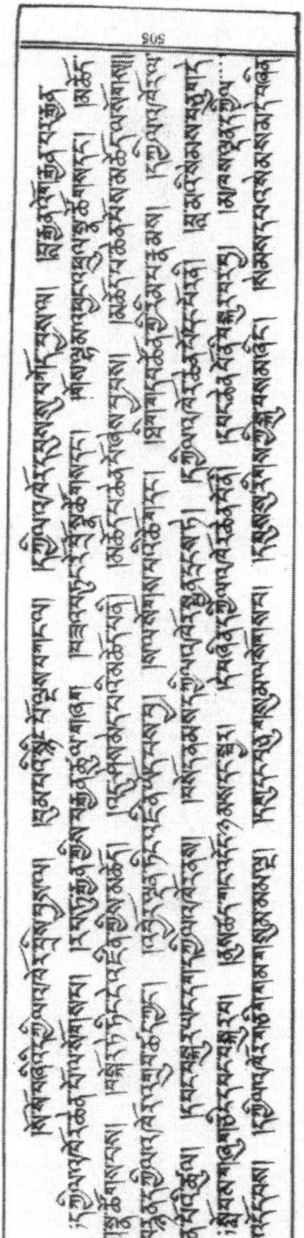

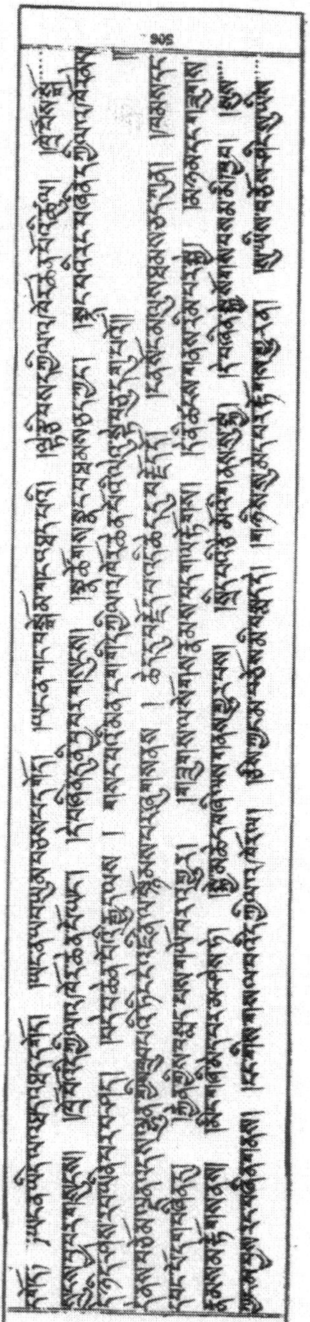

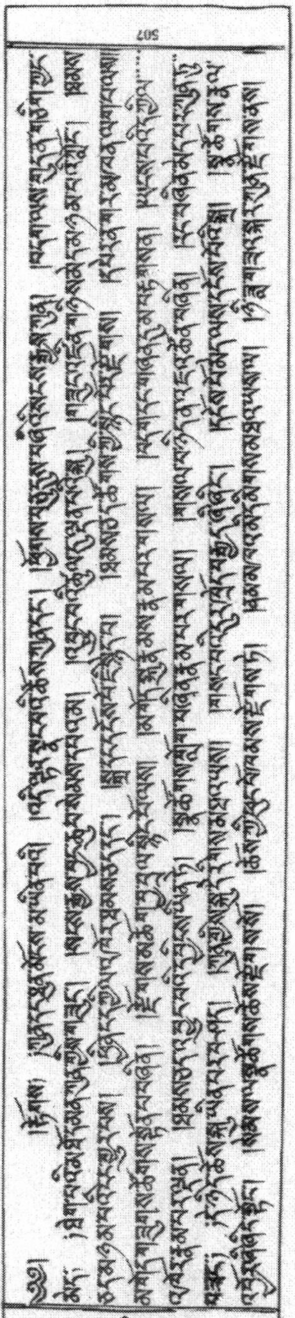
507

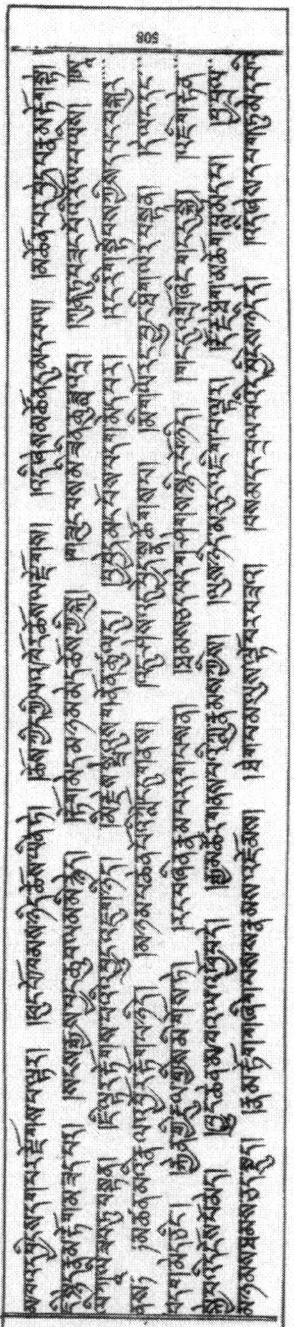
508

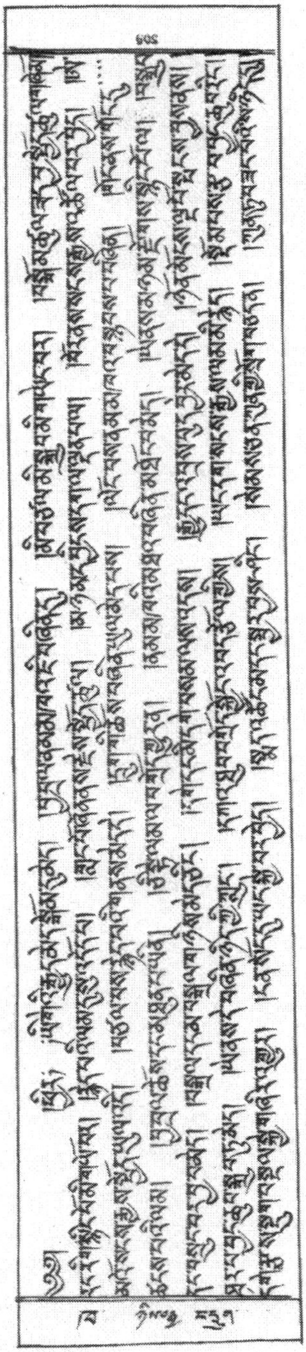

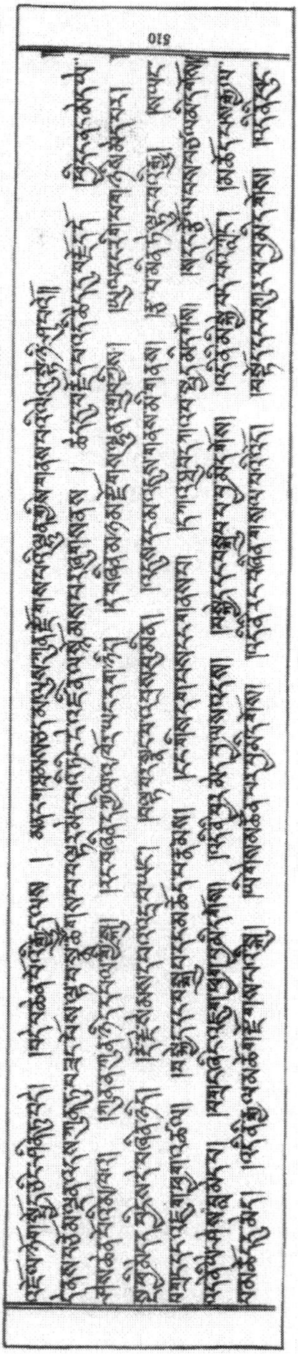

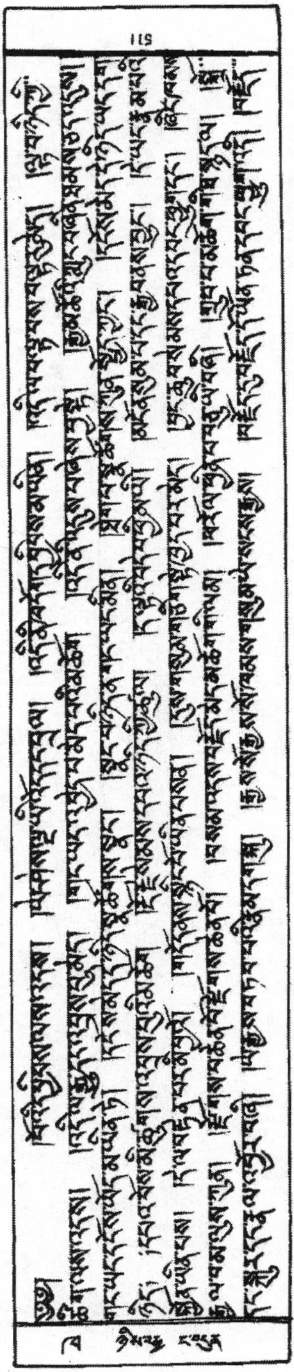

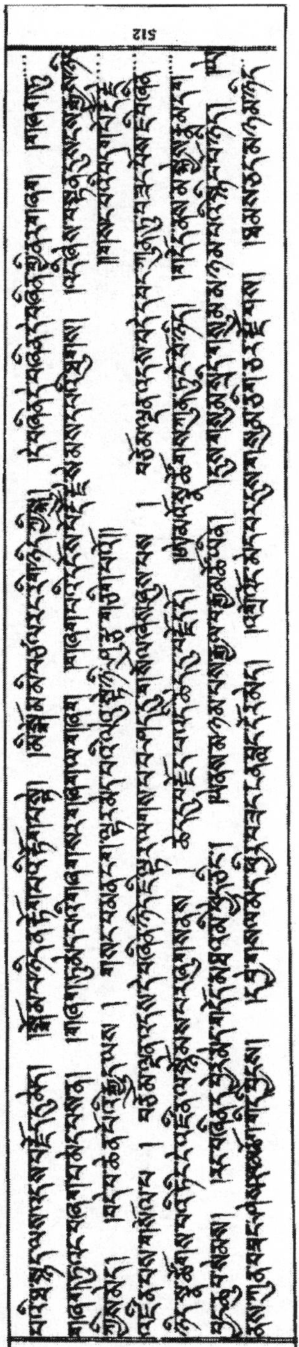

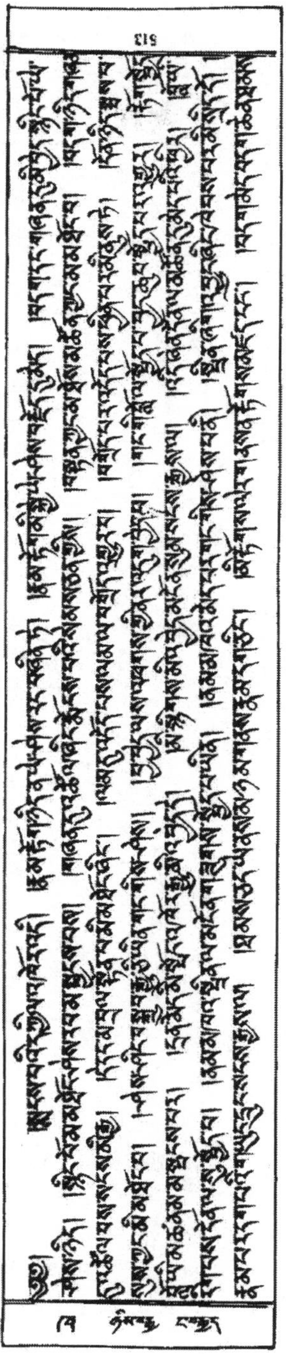

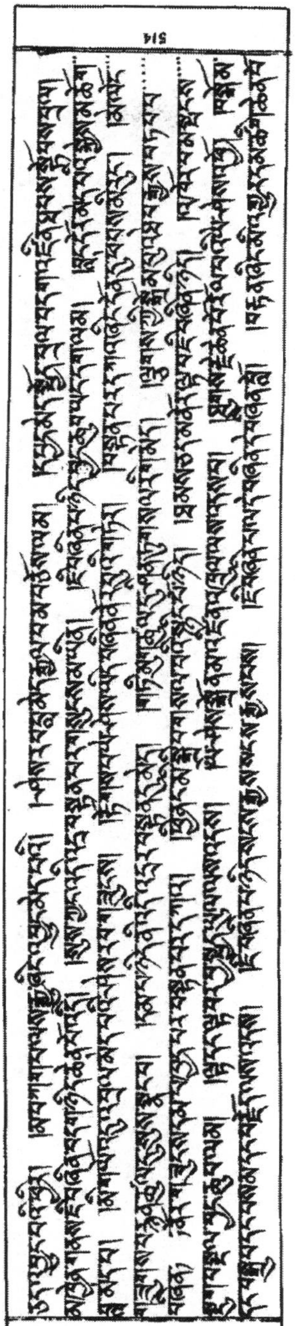

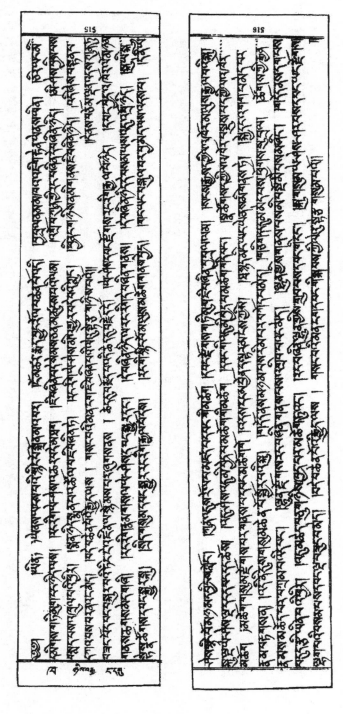

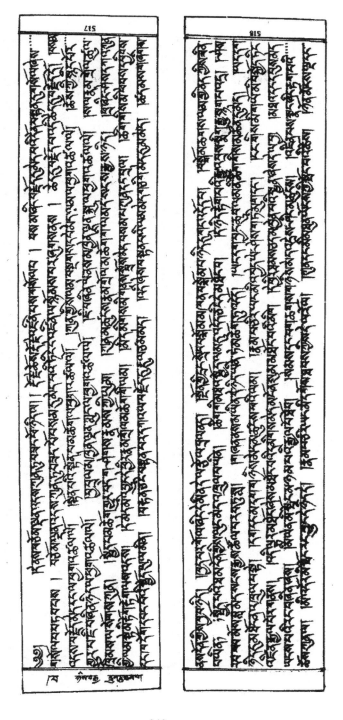

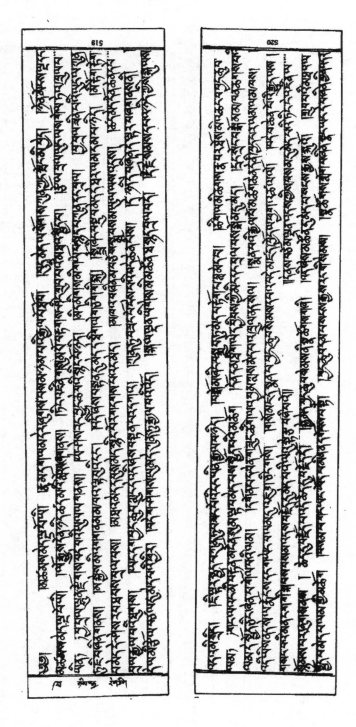

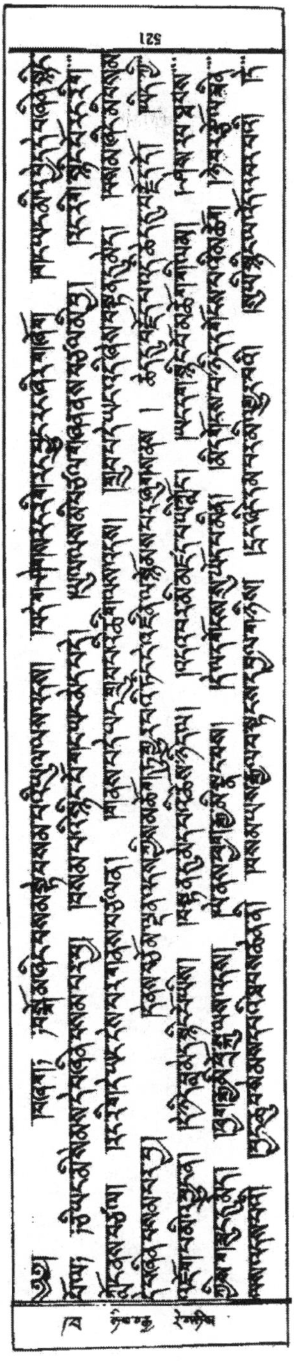
521

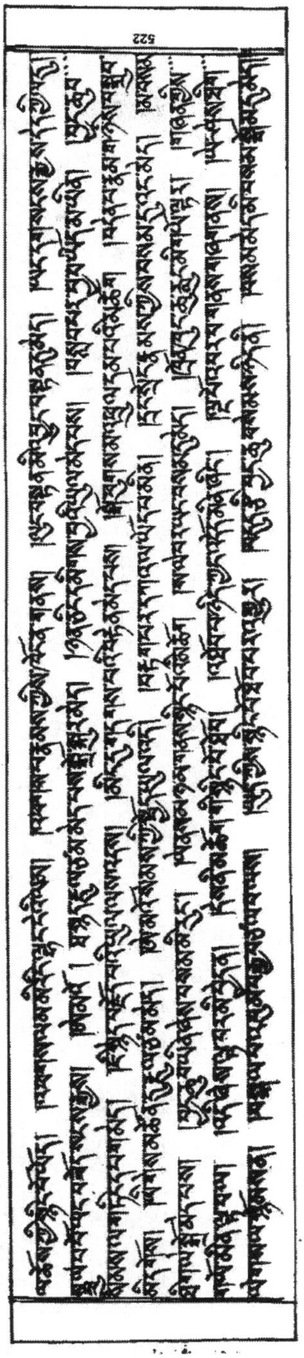
522

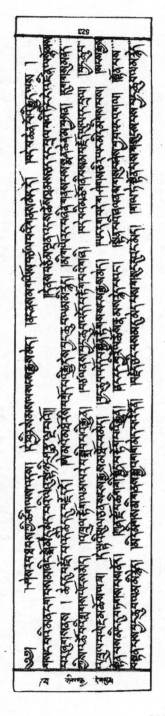

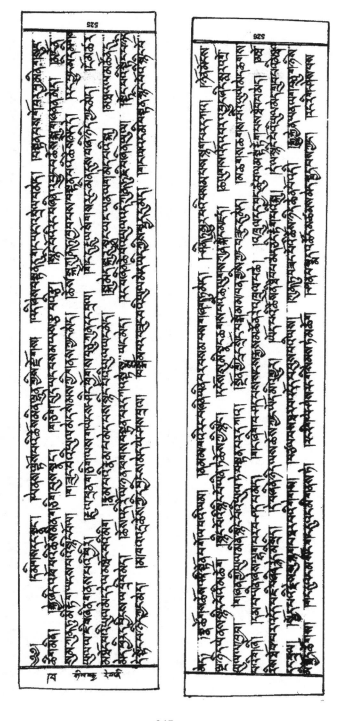

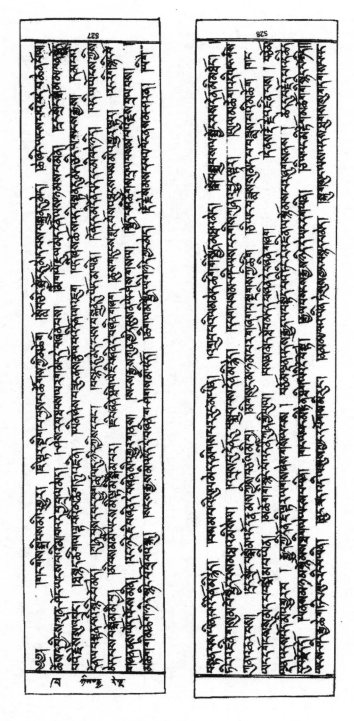

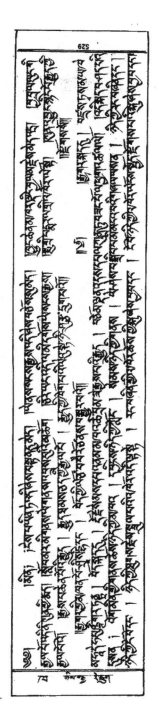

THE TANTRA OF THE NATURAL INTENT OF THE HEART

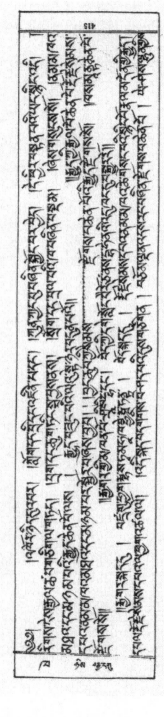

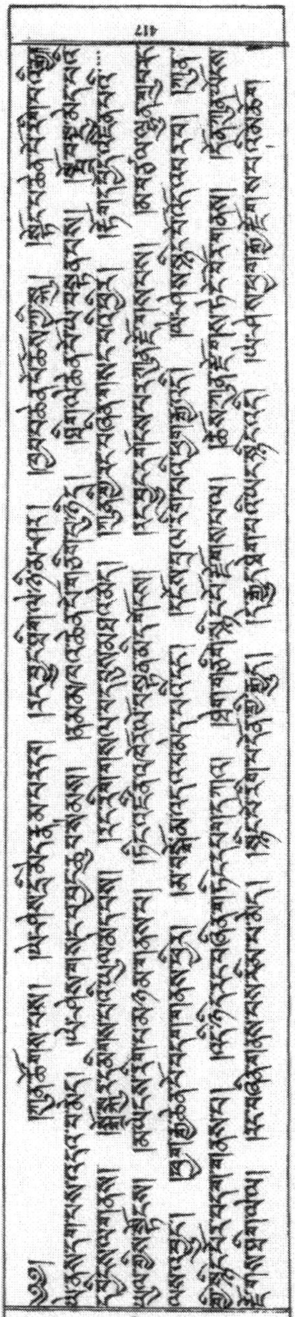

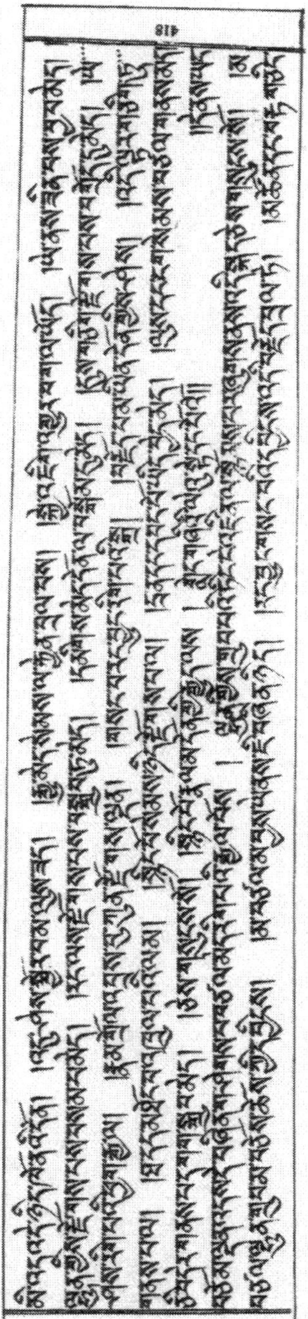

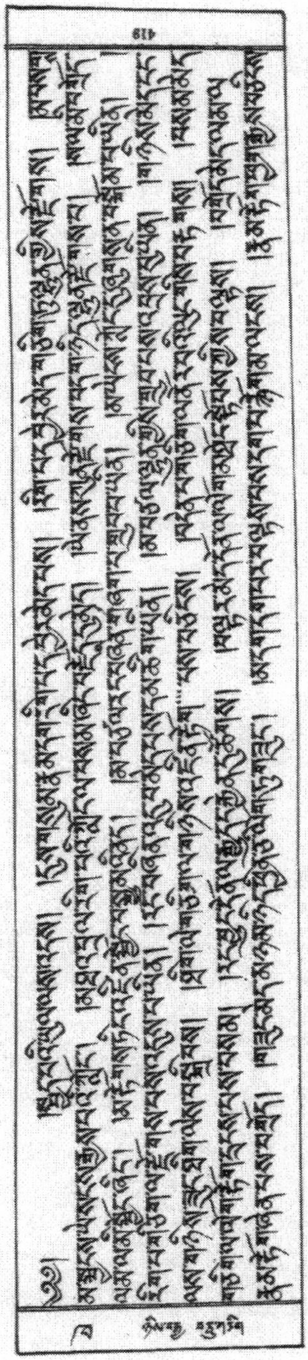

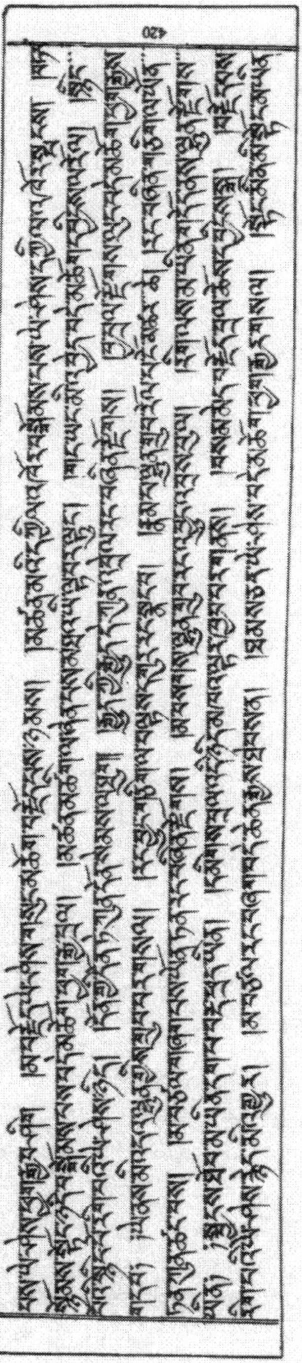

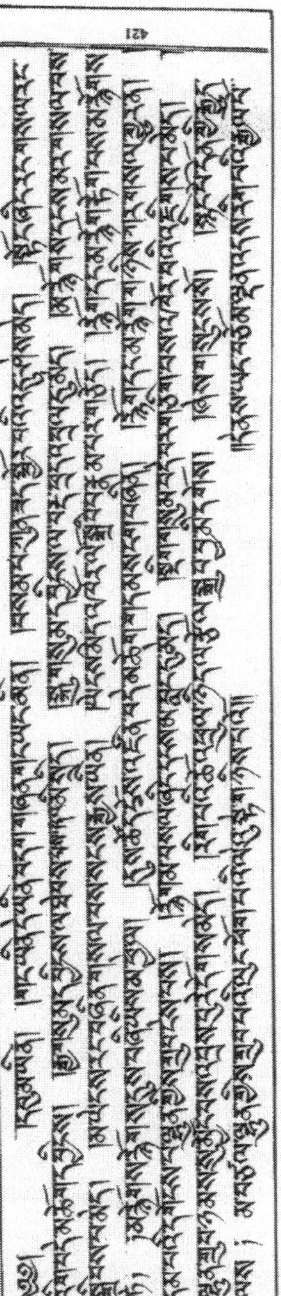

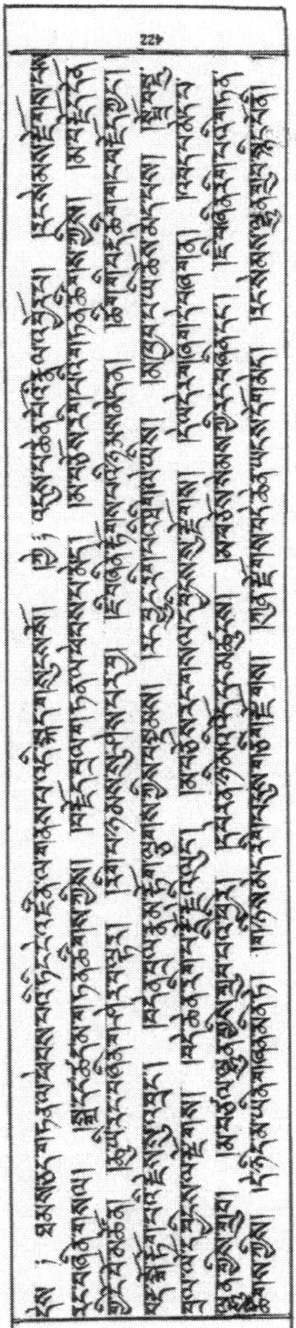

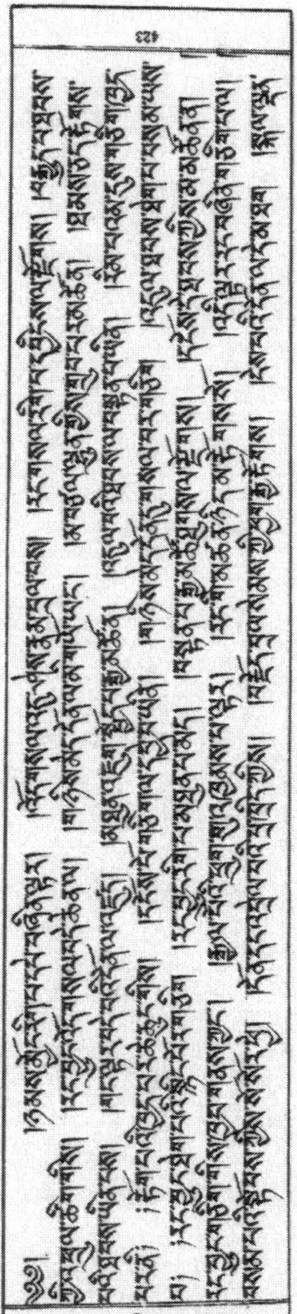

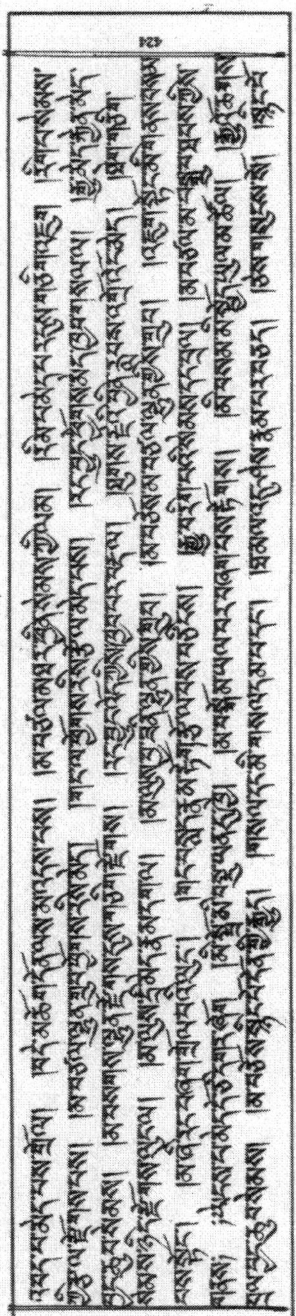

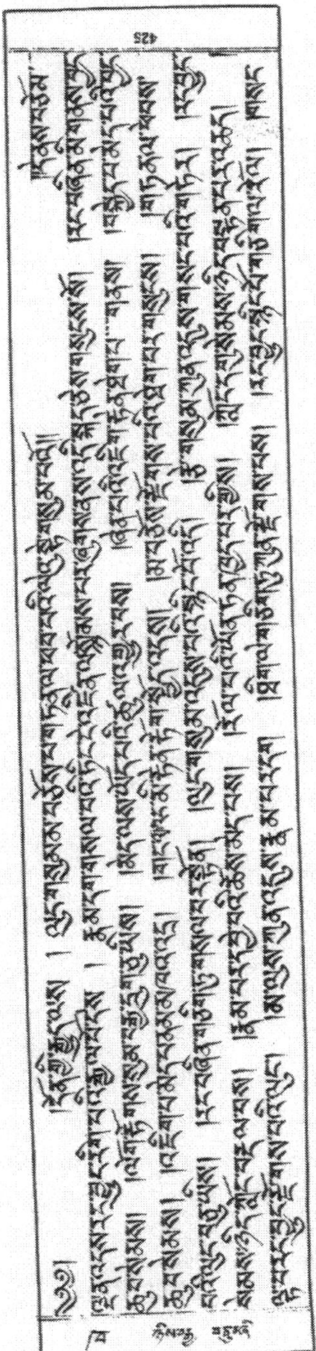

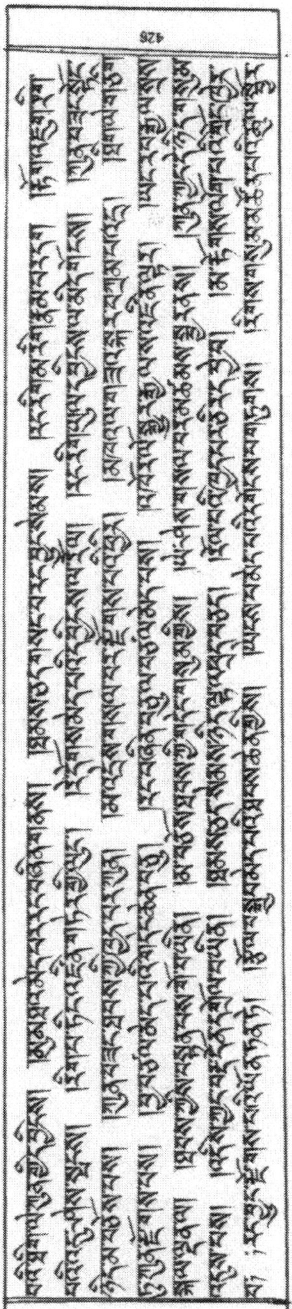

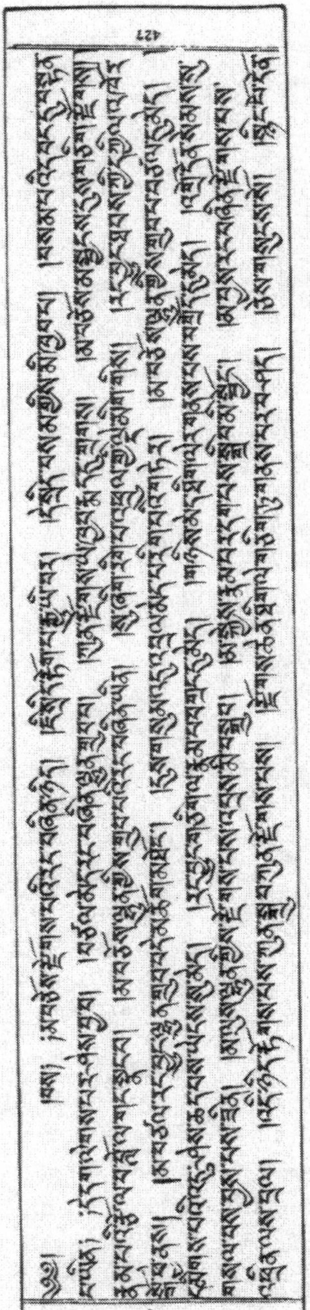

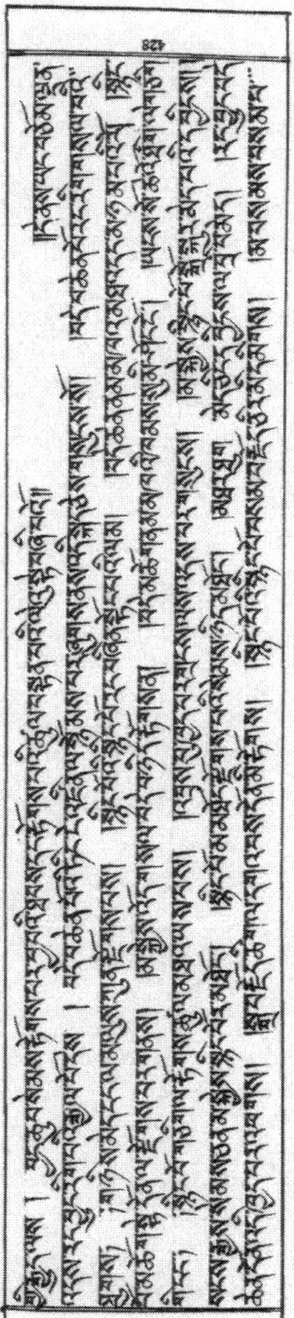

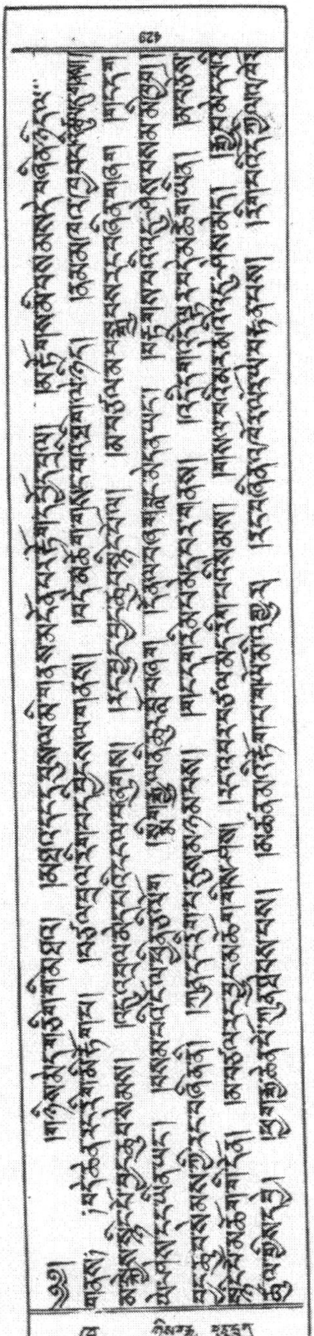

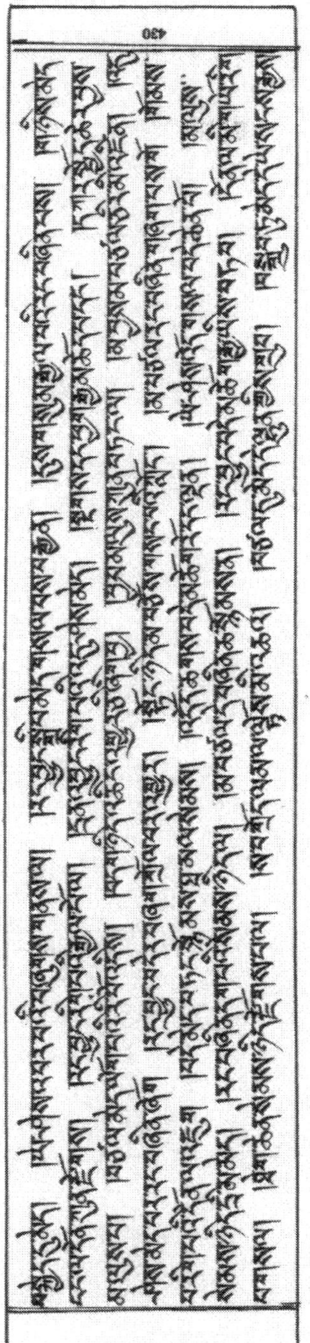

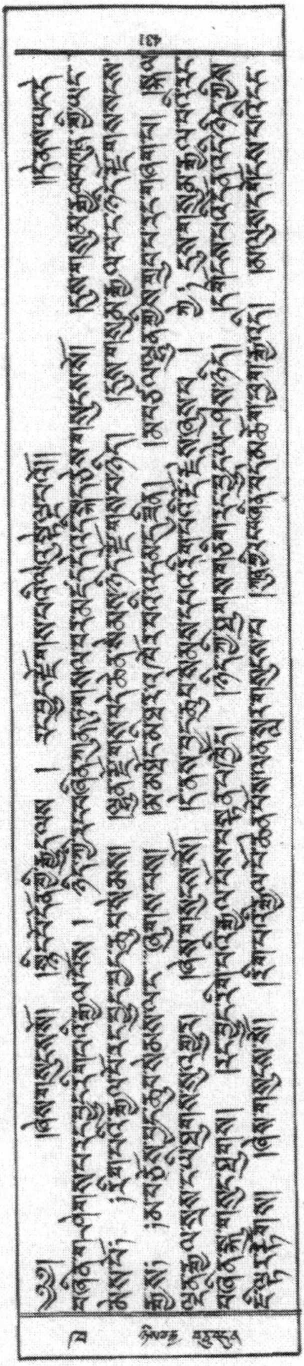

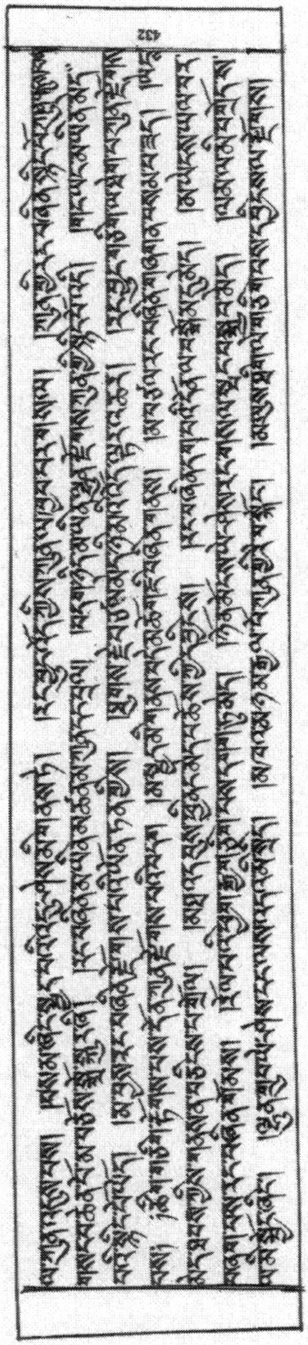

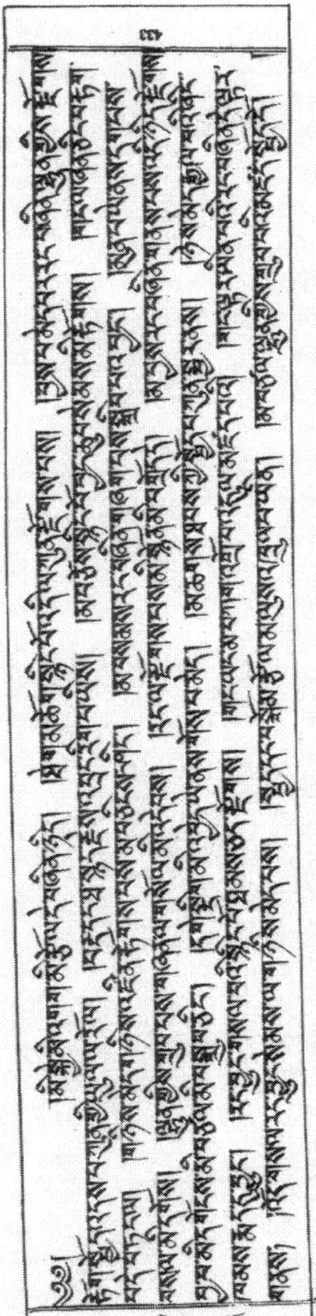

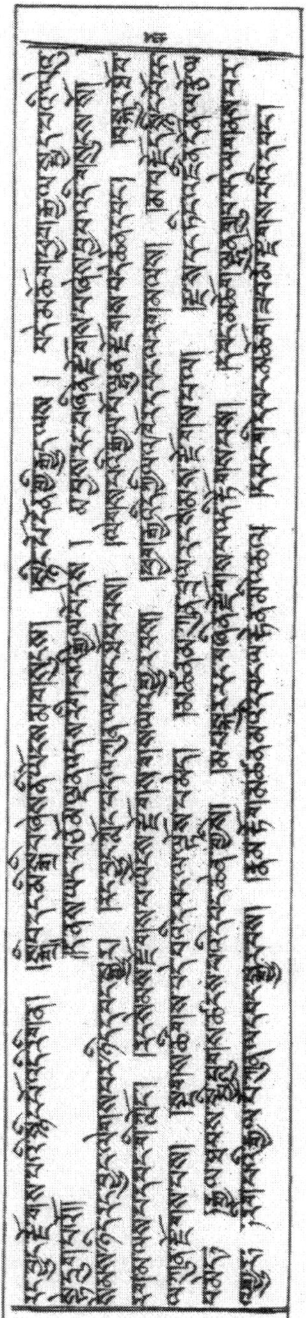

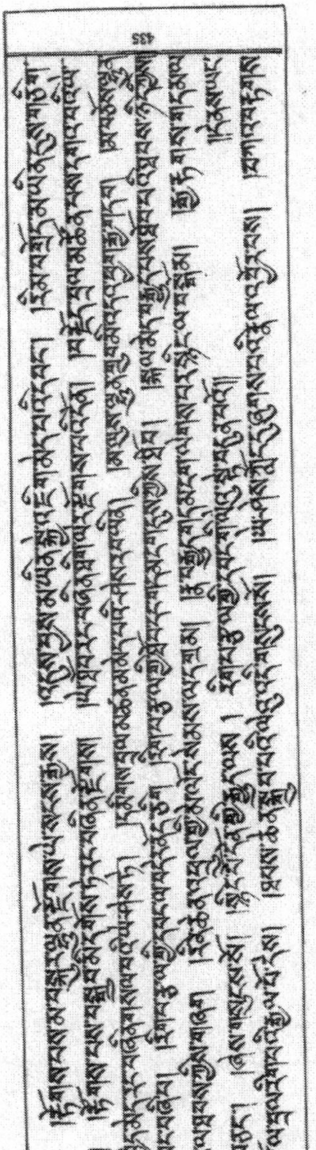

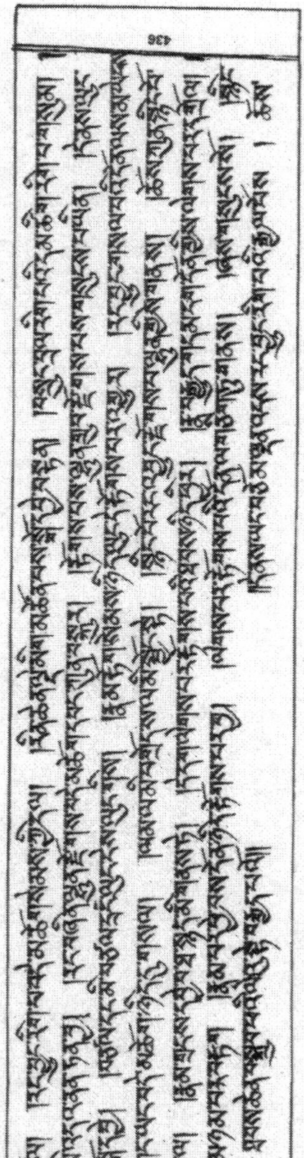

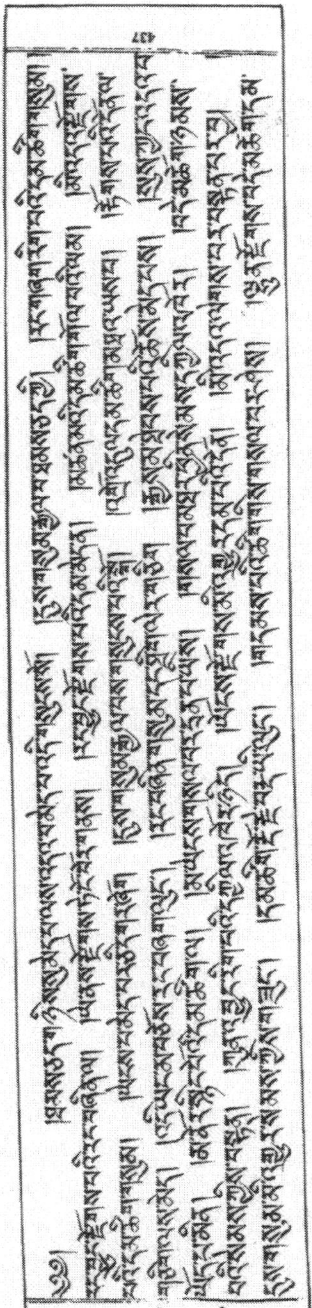

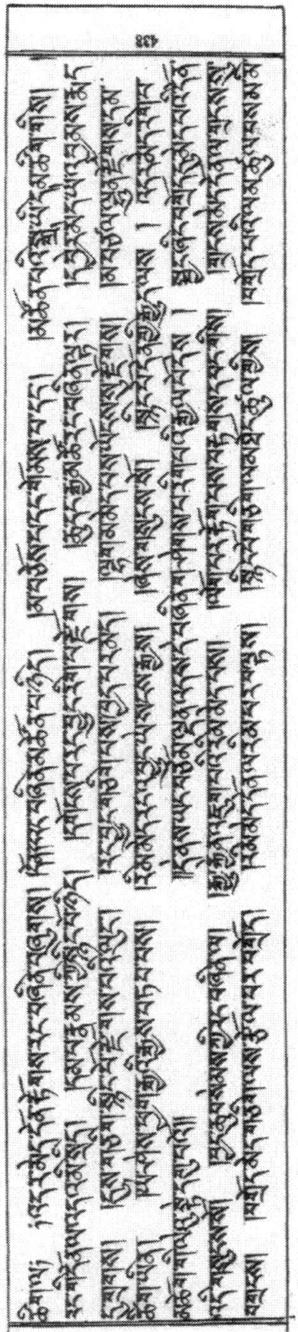

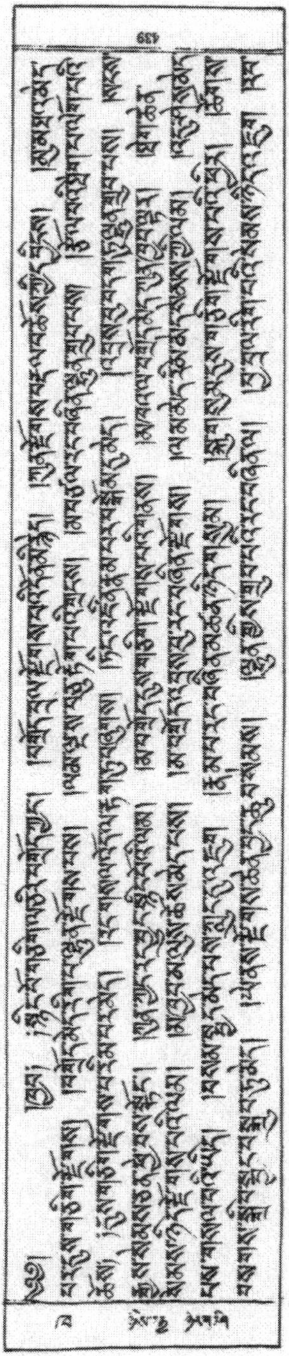
439

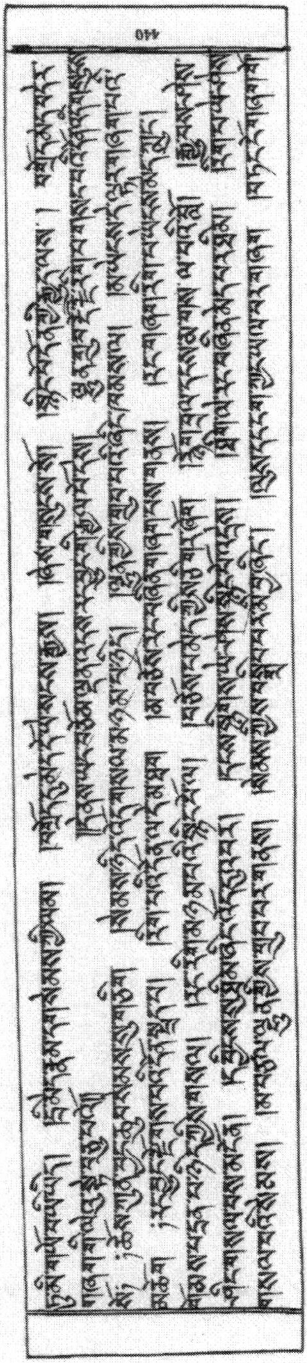
440

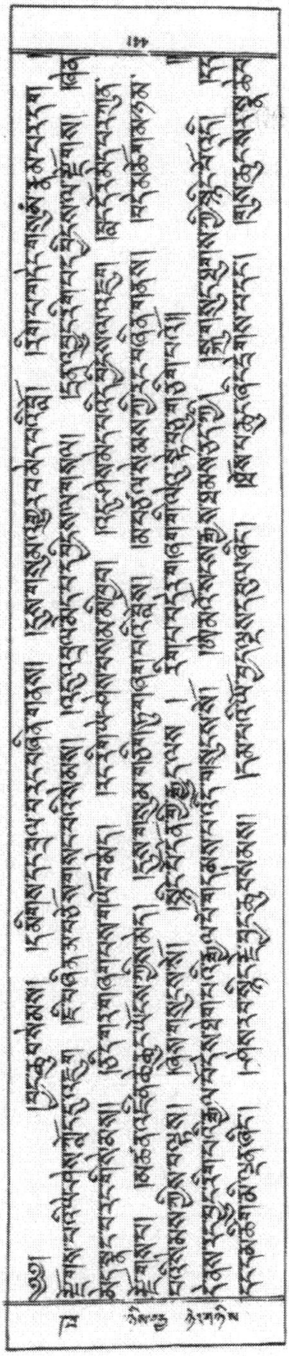

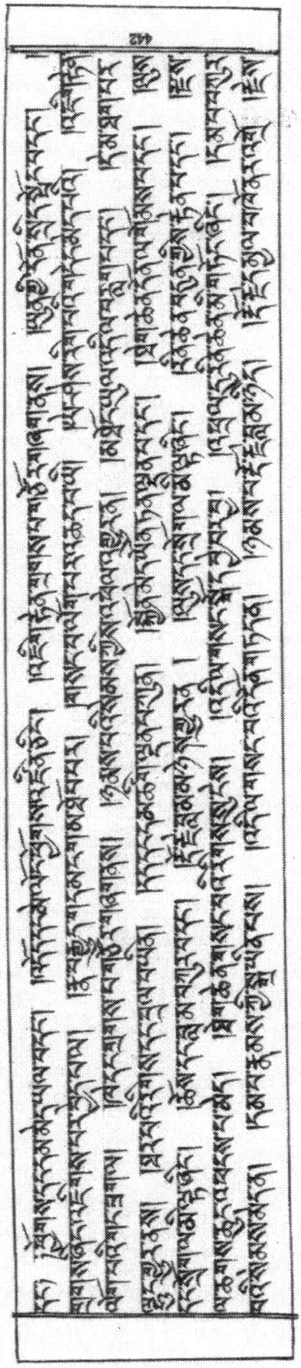

ABOUT THE TRANSLATOR

Christopher Wilkinson began his career in Buddhist literature at the age of fifteen, taking refuge vows from his guru Dezhung Rinpoche. In that same year he began formal study of Tibetan language at the University of Washington under Geshe Ngawang Nornang and Turrell Wylie. He became a Buddhist monk, for three years, at the age of eighteen, living in the home of Dezhung Rinpoche while he continued his studies at the University of Washington. He graduated in 1980 with a B.A. degree in Asian Languages and Literature and another B.A. degree in Comparative Religion (College Honors, Magna Cum Laude, Phi Beta Kappa). After a two year tour of Buddhist pilgrimage sites throughout Asia he worked in refugee resettlement programs for five years in Seattle, Washington. He then proceeded to the University of Calgary for an M.A. in Buddhist Studies where he wrote a groundbreaking thesis on the Yangti transmission of the Great Perfection tradition titled "Clear Meaning: Studies on a Thirteenth Century rDzog chen Tantra." He proceeded to work on a critical edition of the Sanskrit text of the 20,000 line Perfection of Wisdom in Berkeley, California, followed by an intensive study of Burmese language in Hawaii. In 1990 he began three years' service as a visiting professor in English Literature in Sulawesi, Indonesia, exploring the remnants of the ancient Sri Vijaya Empire there. He worked as a research fellow for the Shelly and Donald Rubin Foundation for several years, playing a part in the early development of the Rubin Museum of Art. In the years that followed he became a Research Fellow at the Centre de Recherches sur les Civilisations de l'Asie Orientale, Collège de France, and taught at the University of Calgary as an Adjunct Professor for five years. He has published several volumes of translations of Tibetan literature, and is currently engaged in further translations of classic Buddhist literature.

Notes to Introduction

[1] See The Great Image: The Life Story of Vairochana the Translator by Ani Jinba Palmo. Shambhala: 2013.

[2] Ibid p. 105

[3] The Great Tantra of Vajrasattva: Equal to the End of the Sky. Translated by Christopher Wilkinson. Create Space: 2015.

[4] See Beyond Secret: The Upadeśa of Vairochana on the Practice of the Great Perfection, Translation by Christopher Wilkinson. Create Space: 2015 p. 118

[5] See "The *Mi nub rgyal mtshan Nam mkha' che* and *the Mahā Ākāśa Kārikās*: Origins and Authenticity" by Christopher Wilkinson in Revue d'Etudes Tibétaines *numéro vingt-quatre — Octobre 2012* p. 23.

[6] rNying ma rgyud 'bum mTshams brag dgon kyi bri ma, National Library, Royal Government of Bhutan, Thimpu, 1982. 46 Vols.

[7] The Rgyud 'bum of Vairocana : A collection of Ancient Tantras and Esoteric Instructions compiled and translated by the 8th century Tibetan Master reproduced from the rare manuscript belonging to Tokden Rinpoche of Gangon by Tashi Y. Tashigangpa. Leh, Ladakh, 1971. 8 Volumes. The Secret Intent of the Heart is in Vol. 2, p. 313-337.

Made in the USA
Middletown, DE
19 October 2016